Barbra Streisand

Biography

My name and my story

I love You!

X.

CONTENTS

PEOPLE

'It is fascinating to me that she is so put down by the media. People who know her love her.'

CIS CORMAN

CHAPTER 1

Barbara embarks on the biggest journey of her life: singer and actress. In the summer of 1959. Barbara sent a résumé to casting directors claiming to be both an actor and a singer. A really unique 8 x 10 glossy was attached. Eddie Blum of the Rodgers and Hammerstein casting office was so taken by the photos that he called her and asked what she looked like in real life.

'What part do you want me to audition for?' she said.

'It's for the musical Sound of Music by Rodgers and Hammerstein,' he explained. 'Yeah?'

'Do you remember the story?'

'Sure!' she exclaimed.

'Well, it's the oldest Von Trapp child, Lisl; the one who falls in love with the Nazi youth movement's boy. 'She's blonde, Christian, and sixteen,' he explained.

'I'd be ideal,' she exclaimed. She went straight to his office to audition for the part. 'I bleached it once, and my mother thought I was a lady.' Blum, who was impressed with her voice, encouraged her to devote more time to singing.

She began voice training with the few funds she had. Her teacher, who she found through an ad in a theatre magazine, had previously sung minor roles in a small opera company and spent full lessons on vocal exercises and voice development. 'I feel like singing comes naturally to me,' Barbara remarked, recalling her lessons and how she was taught to produce sounds. 'It's an extension of speaking on a higher level,' she says. The singing lessons, which she had found upsetting due to her chronic ear condition, ended abruptly.

The clicks and buzzing she had once heard in her ears had developed into a high-pitched noise, not a spasmodic, but constant ringing. She didn't hear the silence. She got her ears checked and was informed about her illness as well as the fact that she possessed supersonic hearing.

This terrible condition influenced how she viewed words, lyrics, and music. She could sense the cadences, the changes in rhythm, and the quiet between beats. She could smoothly transition from deeper chest sounds to higher pitched head sounds, a skill that takes years of musical study to master. At the same time, because she heard things more clearly and forcefully than most musicians, when she sang, she was aware of every minor flaw in her voice. She rarely listened to the radio because the fidelity was poor on the primitive machines she had access to, causing her to focus on the flaws.

Shortly after the tum down by Eddie Blum, she cashed her last unemployment check and joined the Actors Co-op, a collection of somewhat desperate out-of-work performers all yearning for an appearance in a legitimate theatre where they would be seen and critiqued. Barry Dennen, a thin, dark-haired, charismatic young actor from Los Angeles, California, was also cast as a cricket and a snail. The two were drawn to each other. Dennen, who had attended UCLA and was several years Barbara's senior, hailed from a well-to-do West Coast Jewish family.

The Lion was a club across the street from where I lived [on West Ninth Street in the Village]. On Thursdays, there was a talent show. If she came in and signed up, I would work with her on a set of songs, assist her in selecting material, and direct her show.' Her terms flipped the order. She would join up if she thought she had a chance following his tutoring. Dennen concurred. He escorted her to The Lion at the end of a week, standing over her as she signed her name as Barbra Streisand on the audition sheet. She then explained that it was not an accident. There were too many Barbaras, and she desired to stand apart. She did, however, want to maintain her last name so that when she got famous, everyone in Brooklyn would recognize her. Dennen had taped her practice sessions and replayed them for her to review. The newly christened Barbra Streisand was certain she was on her way to glory, which spurred her to rehearse at breakneck speed for the audition, not stopping until both of them were too fatigued to continue.

5

Dennen was in love with her, but he also recognized her uniqueness and huge untapped talent. His desire to turn her into a professional performer, which she had not been when they first started working together, was nearly obsessive.

Despite realising how much Dennen may contribute to her future, she never seemed thankful. Dennen had not anticipated her presence. She had fallen in love with herself, and he believed it was a quality that would benefit her performance. Her compensation was whatever satisfaction he felt from assisting her transformation into an intriguing performance. Dennen's tremendous assistance and support were viewed by Barbra as a little measure of restitution for all the years of being put down by Diana, which she felt was due from someone she loved.

Dennen has now suggested to her that she move in with him. The decision was not tough because they had grown unusually close and she had been evicted from her previous flat. She was not only emotionally and financially reliant on him, but she was also in love with him. They started dating while she was preparing for her audition at The Lion. Dennen was her first true affair and the first man she had lived with, despite her attraction to other young men during her early Village days. She hadn't given up her primary aim of being an actor, but she was now confident that it was feasible if she could establish herself as a singer who also happened to be an actress. Phrasing, material selection, and putting together a class act were all necessary, and her instincts told her that Dennen might help.

She was ready at the end of this intense week of metamorphosis. They both thought the talent show would lead to her debut as a cabaret performer. The competition was held on a hot, airless evening on July 2, 1960. Barbra had turned eighteen in April of the previous year. She appeared to be a few years older.

Dennen was at The Lion every evening during her two-week run, taking notes on her performance and the reactions of the audience. And he'd collaborate with her on new figures. 'I would choose material that was fantastic musically and would show off her voice, as well as songs that were unique, forgotten, or crazy,' Dennen explains. It was my idea to have her play "Who's Afraid of the Big

Bad Wolf?" in front of New York's most sophisticated and astute audience.'

Her two-week stint at The Lion ended on July 16. The top New York cabarets would be closed for the month of August. She waited impatiently as the sweltering late summer days stripped Manhattan of most of its glitz. Heat steamed up from the walkways, trapped between the high-rise tunnels. The streets smelled strongly of burnt rubber and baked-in garbage. The fire brigade turned on the fire hydrants in the poor areas so that the kids could cool themselves by darting in and out of the water. Those who could packed their weekend bags and headed out to the country. Barbra stayed in town, barely leaving Dennen's flat.

On a sweltering Sunday evening in late July, she auditioned for the Bon Soir. 'This is the start of something,' she reflected on the walk to the club with Dennen, Schulenberg, and Bark McHugh, an elderly off-Broadway producer Dennen knew who was also a scout for emerging cabaret talent and had arranged the audition. When a cool breeze blew in, she felt a chill run through her entire body. She recalls feeling different and more confident in herself that evening. She walked so quickly that the men had trouble keeping up with her.

The Bon Soir was a cellar club run by the Mafia. The homosexual bar at the back of the one enormous space it filled existed as a result of policy concessions. The Tiger Haynes Trio, each member a spectacular solo musician, and Mae Barnes, a "five-by-five singer with dark saucer eyes, a grainy powerhouse voice, and the sassiest good-time spirit ever to haunt a night-club stage," were among the club's regular performers. It was also a major showcase for up-and-coming white entertainers such as Kaye Ballard, Phyllis Diller, and Dick Cavett.

They entered through a back entrance that led down a steep, barely lighted flight of steps, as the club was closed on Sundays. The area was almost completely dark. The managers and a few employees occupied only a few tables. One overhead light was turned on. Tiger Haynes, a respected guitarist, watched her from across the room as she approached the accompanist, Englishman Peter Daniels, and discussed the music she had just handed him - 'A Sleepin' Bee' -

before going up on the narrow platform and adjusting the microphone. Her demeanour was one of authority. The Bon Soir was several times the size of The Lion, and despite being in the Village, it had a reputation that drew New York's most refined uptown cabaret-goers to its cellar doors on Eighth Street.

Her normal 'bizarre' clothing was replaced by a basic, sleeveless brown cotton dress due to the extreme heat. Her hair was piled high on the crown of her head. She insisted on a blue spotlight rather than a pink one, and the result was stunning. She resembled a Modigliani picture. The instant she began to sing, a shock shot through the darkened, silent chamber, a spine-tingling urgency behind every note. Her tone was clear and strong, and her wording was superb. It was an incredible performance. She sang to the practically empty room as if every chair was occupied and the phantom people were attentively listening to her. The enchantment in her voice was palpable. 'It looks good,' Bark McHugh said when she was done. Tiger Haynes' girlfriend, Bea, approached Streisand and said, 'Little kid, you got cash signs written all over you!'

'Yeah? 'Do you truly believe that?' she asked, smiling. 'Perhaps you can inform management.'

Her remuneration for a two-week engagement was $108 per week. She was gonna be the featured performer only. The main attraction was comedian Phyllis Diller. 'Hey!' exclaimed Barbra to one of her friends. 'This is just the start. The stakes will be bigger next time, and the venue will be more upscale.'

'It's strange,' Bob Schulenberg admitted, 'since I always imagined Barry would be the legend and Barbra the cabaret performer.' The two men originally met on the set of an amateur film Dennen had written while they were both students at UCLA. 'He was a fantastic performer, very bright. He performed Les Fourberies de Scapin, which I designed, at UCLA, and his French was so good that everyone assumed he was French. He's a fantastic entertainer. A visionary and a perfectionist. He constantly added something fresh to the roles he performed.'

Schulenberg had previously worked as an assistant art director for Berman Costumes in Hollywood, as well as designing for the Ice Capades. He'd come to New York to begin work as an art director for the firm of West, Weir, and Bartell, where - as fate would have it - Shelley was now employed. 'I liked him a lot, but I got the impression he was a little embarrassed by Barbra, at least at the time.' Schulenberg, a huge fan of both modern and legendary cabaret acts, was blown away by Barbra when he first heard her sing. He also believed that appropriate make-up would improve her appearance significantly.

'She was really young, and she didn't look horrible, but I guess she thought she did,' says the author. Schulenberg remembered. 'It was heartbreaking because I knew how badly she wanted to appear attractive but didn't know how to pull it off. She had a remarkable face, beautiful eyes, and an Egyptian-like profile. I thought she was beautiful and that I could help her, but it was a difficult, delicate situation. I pondered about it for a long time and eventually did a simple drawing of her without makeup to analyse her face shape.'

Schulenberg saw Barbra more frequently in August, when Dennen was rehearsing for the Central Park staging of Measure for Measure. He gradually persuaded her that she needed a make-up makeover while they were roaming around the Village. They were going to Dennen's opening night together, and it looked like the perfect opportunity. Schulenberg arrived at the apartment early, armed with theatrical make-up equipment. 'She had beautiful eyes and a lovely face. I created cheekbones where there was still baby fat, contoured her eyes, feathered some synthetic eyelashes shorter than her own, and lengthened the line at the corner of her eyelids. I explained what I was doing and why I was doing it to her at each step. Because she didn't have deep-set eyes, she had to force it. The double layer of eyelashes contributed to this impression. I used heavy grease paint to conceal her skin problem scars.'

She kept staring at herself in the mirror, moving her face in different directions and mumbling exasperated remarks. 'I see! I see! Hey! 'Not bad, is it?' She was overjoyed, ecstatic about the transformation.

Streisand and Schulenberg were so preoccupied with Barbra's makeover that they arrived at Measure to Measure too late to see Dennen perform. He was extremely hurt, and while they continued to live together, their relationship had taken a turn for the worse. Dennen assisted her with the act she was about to do at the Bon Soir, focusing on the dramatic presentation. Streisand now had a clear idea of how she wanted to sound and what she wanted to sing, including great Harold Arlen songs like 'When the Sun Comes Out,' Fats Waller's 'Keepin' Out of Mischief Now,' and the childlike 'Who's Afraid of the Big Bad Wolf?' which she turned into a campy, lively, and raunchy interpretation. They were all part of her new act, which would revolve around the idea of a young girl's passage from tease to love awakening to lost love and adulthood - each song performed as a mini-drama under Dennen's supervision. She was strong-willed and always striving to be at the top of her game. She was wise enough to embrace outside ideas when she recognized their value, and she worked relentlessly to absorb and adapt whatever he could give to her performance.

She practised her 'look' with equal zeal with Schulenberg. He created a portrait of Barbra with half of her face done up and the other part left unaltered. She'd then take the drawing and all of her make-up into the bathroom and carefully try to fill in the blank side of the picture on her face so that the two parts matched. When it didn't work, she'd scrub her face clean and start over, sometimes four or five times, a process that often took several hours.

Streisand was the centre of an odd triangle, badgered and disciplined by two young men desperate to see her flourish - a Brooklyn Eliza Doolittle. However, things are not always as they look. Barbra Streisand's desire to achieve was stronger than her mentors'. She would have had less time for them if they had been less talented or unable to assist her in achieving her goals. It wasn't that she was unappreciative. Streisand was in a hurry to get to her target, and she welcomed whatever Dennen and Schulenberg could offer to help her develop as a performer.

She thought she loved Dennen, but her only previous experience with an intimate male-female relationship was her mother's terrible marriage to Kind. Dennen provided her with affection and approval, as well as an alliance in which she was the centre of attention. What more could she possibly want from a man or an affair?

CHAPTER 2

She walked on stage to a packed house on Friday, September 9, 1960, wearing a brown wool-jersey thrift-shop dress, a matching cloche hat from the twenties, and a pair of spike-heeled, ankle-strap shoes. As she tiptoed across the shadowy stage to the microphone set up in front of a high seat, ice cubes clinked in glasses as people conversed. The audience assumed she was a comedian after the spotlight picked her up while she was already seated.

A terrifying wave swept over her. These were tough, uptown types who would compare her to the current top cabaret entertainers: Julie Wilson, Anita Ellis, Felicia Sanders, Portia Nelson, and the sultry-voiced Julie London. She took a deep breath and began singing 'A Sleepin' Bee' in a quiet hum, the microphone one inch from her mouth. It was a daring start. Most cabaret acts began with a lively piece to pique the audience's interest. Her voice became louder a few moments into the song, and she extended her arm and open-palmed her hand where the bee was supposed to be sleeping. People turned to look at her. People in their chairs leaned forward. She could sense the audience's interest. They erupted in applause when she finished the song and were fully hers when she cut their answer short and surged into 'When the Sun Comes Out' as if she were heralding the eclipse of Western civilisation'.

'When she went off the stage, she was in a kind of trance,' comic and impressionist Larry Storch, who was also making his way in the cabaret industry, said. I went to express my congratulations to her. "Kid, you are going to be a very great star!" I think I remarked. After performing those solemn songs, they pulled her back on stage, and she performed "Who's Afraid of the Big Bad Wolf?" That was really nicely thought out! What a brilliant idea! It simply killed everyone. They forced her to sing it three times. It was amazing. It felt like something out of A Star Is Born.'

The welcome Streisand received was overwhelming. As she ended her act, she had tears in her eyes and appeared overheated. More than just her talent had been recognized. Barbra Streisand had only recently discovered her ability to command an audience.

She became more relaxed after a few concerts and would talk to the crowd between songs - not much, just to introduce her bandmates. BonSoir increased her weekly wage to $125 and prolonged her contract for an additional eleven weeks. Streisand was keen to better her performance during that time. Her lifelong fixation with excellence in all she did had begun in earnest, as had the committed work ethic she inherited from her father. Dennen came in his tape recorder and meticulously documented her act for the first two weeks. Later on, they would go over each number, changing the phrasing, the placement of particular tunes, and the back-up sound. At the end of that time, he delegated her care to Bob Schulenberg and left to visit his family in California, issuing a final directive that she not call him there because he had not yet discussed their situation with his parents.

Streisand was offended by his dictatorial behaviour, but she agreed to his terms. 'He genuinely cares about me,' she explained to Schulenberg. 'He'll tell his parents about us when he's ready.'

They repeated the operation the next night, and Dennen was still missing when they returned to the residence. Dennen remained silent for several days. She was nervous, emotional, and enraged at the same time. 'After a week, I suppose Barbra ate up all her emotion for Barry,' Schulenberg continues. He eventually returned, and she remained calm. "Hi, how was your trip?" she asked. Is your family well? Great — I'm still singing at the Bon Soir."

She stayed at Dennen's apartment, suppressing her rage and rising hate toward him. She blamed him for the loss of the flame. He was embarrassed and rejected her. In a short period of time, she would be able to erase all conscious recollection of his significant contribution to her development as a performer while clinging to the injury she imagined she had sustained at his hands. She couldn't entirely let go because she still needed Dennen's guidance, but she began to rely more on Peter Daniels, her accompanist, who was now arranging her new material and with whom she had formed an emotional bond. There was no sexual relationship this time, and she was in charge. She was gaining in regard to her own taste, which had been fashioned by Dennen but was now a reflection of herself.

She finally left Dennen's apartment after a heated disagreement over the dozens of tapes he had made of her voice, rehearsals, and performances over the six months they had been dating. Dennen refused to give her the master tapes. They felt like they belonged to Streisand and her voice. Dennen was not convinced. He was the one who started, directed, and recorded the cassettes. Neither would give in, and they parted on a harsh, unpleasant note. Dennen described the records as "like children in a divorce." 'They stood for a lot of things. We split up as lovers who were both heartbroken and misunderstood.'

The tour would take her by train to places such as Detroit, Cleveland, and St. Louis, among others. 'She was half excited and half terrified,' Schulenberg says. 'It was gonna be her first trip away from New York. Finally, on the day she was to depart, we loaded her belongings into a taxi and drove to the train station. Suddenly, she asked if she may get out of the vehicle and go to the drugstore... She was late, and I knew she'd miss the train if we stopped, so I asked her directly what she needed. "Do you think they have toothpaste in Detroit?" she blurted out, showing her anxiety of the unknown she faced, possibly attempting to prolong or postpone it.

Once in Detroit, she devised an exotic story to tell the press in order to make herself appear more interesting: she was born in Turkey. The local press dubbed her "the Turkish-born, Brooklyn-raised songstress in a hurry, with a completely untrained but remarkably true voice."

She assumed that appearing on one of the major television discussion shows would hasten her ascension to heady glory, and she began to contact and haunt the various programme bookers. 'I turned down Barbra Streisand,' said Bob Shanks, talent coordinator for the Tonight Show, which aired nationwide every weeknight.[3] Streisand would not accept his negative attitude and continued to contact. 'Everyone in the industry says you're so sensitive and sympathetic about talent that I have to talk to you,' she explained. 'I need your help.'

She then stated emphatically that her mother was terminally ill in Cleveland and desperately wanted her to return home to marry a childhood sweetheart she did not love. 'If you could just give me one chance so she could see me on the Tonight Show, it would keep me here and establish my career,' she cried, and Shanks was taken in.

'Paar [who thought she was too blatantly Jewish in appearance and demeanour] didn't think she was fit for his show,' Shanks explains. But, as fate would have it, Orson Bean, who had seen her at the Bon Soir and been blown away by her skill, was scheduled to take over as guest presenter for Paar on 5 April and agreed to hire her. She cancelled her appointment in Detroit and flew to New York, half-afraid because she had never flown before, to appear on her first national television show. Phyllis Diller also appeared on the show. She sang 'A Sleepin' Bee' and then moved over to sit between Diller and Bean, looking fresh and young in a short, slim black dress with spaghetti shoulder straps - an ensemble advised by Schulenberg who reminded her that simple and elegant were also attention grabbers.

'This is so thrilling,' she exclaimed, her modish dress trailing several inches above her voluptuous crossed legs. 'All of these people, cameras, lights, and people!' She came across as a naive, natural Brooklyn weirdo, and the audience liked her for it.

Her televised debut boosted her self-esteem. She felt more at ease performing in front of the camera and not having to worry about a critical cabaret audience. This relieved her anxiety, and she spoke glibly, sounding weird but endearing. She was essentially playing herself. This allowed her to focus just on the aspects of her personality that she believed would make an engaging character, and she was correct.

Immediately after the Tonight Show she flew back to Detroit and then moved on to St Louis, from where she wrote Barry Dennen a businesslike letter asking him to email her the guitar chords he had arranged for 'A Taste of Honey'. She suggested that perhaps he could come up with a replacement for 'Lover Come Back to Me' as her act's closing number.

He responded to her request by recommending 'Cry Me a River,' a sombre song recorded by Julie London. She returned to New York with records of her appearances on local radio stations throughout her trip. 'We went over them as we had previously,' Dennen adds. 'I instructed her how to polish her performance, what songs to put in her repertoire: they were essentially the tunes she would later perform on her first album. She came to my apartment one day in May 1961 and we recorded "A Taste of Honey." It was not an easy reunion. 'We both felt bitter, misunderstood, and sad,' Dennen explained. The love affair ended. They visited each other on occasion during the next few months, encounters arranged by Streisand, who sought his help on musical arrangements. She then abruptly quit calling.

'Barbra adored Barry, but it was much more than that,' claims Schulenberg. 'She admired him as a teacher and motivator. She was devastated when things didn't work out between them. She reacted by refusing to listen to anyone's counsel.'

She returned to the Bon Soir shortly after her tour, including 'Cry Me a River' in her act, twisting the original concept of 'a repentant lover who had come back for a second chance' into a story about a once-scorned woman demanding tears of loss from the man who had involved her in a hurting relationship. 'When I sang it,' she subsequently revealed, 'I was thinking of one particular individual; I attempted to reproduce in my mind the nuances of his face.'4 Mr. Barry Dennen.

Without a doubt, Streisand owed a lot to Dennen, but she was equally driven to succeed. She would have undoubtedly won without Dennen's guidance. Nonetheless, he aided her in accelerating her progress. She no longer needed him after her transmogrification, and she did not treat him well in the future when they met. 'When she's done with you, she's done with you,' observed another close colleague. 'When her desire for you fades, so does the connection.'

BROADWAY BABY

'She was the most innocent thing I'd ever seen, like a beautiful flower that hasn't bloomed yet. But she was so strange that I was afraid.'

ELLIOTT GOULD

CHAPTER 3

Barbra Streisand had arrived on Broadway at the age of ninety-nine. Her initiation would be difficult. Almost the whole cast of I Can Get It for You Wholesale have prior experience. Elliott, on the other hand, felt she looked great and was fascinated by her eclecticism. They didn't meet until the first day of rehearsals, in which she went in a ragged black coat from the 1930s that reached her ankles, the sleeves pushed back so her hands could show, and a turn-of-the-century black medical satchel bag functioning as a purse. Of course, this was not true, but Elliott viewed her through fresh amorous eyes. She wasn't a lady he wanted to transform, nor was she a performer he wanted to shape. He adored her eccentricity, naturalness, and voracious appetite for food, people, and new experiences. She was immediately drawn to him. He stood out, but he didn't appear to be her ideal leading guy. His clothes, whether custom-tailored or ready-made, never quite suited him since he was tall (six feet, three inches), thick, with dark bushy hair and ethnic features. He could do a dance with astonishing ease when called upon, yet he was always stumbling on and off stage.

She landed her first role as Fanny Brice after much hunting and convincing. On 3 October, she travelled to Los Angeles in high spirits, intending to announce her casting as Fanny Brice on The Judy Garland Show. Her positive attitude persisted upon her return to New York, as she anticipated the next stage in her career - the lead in a Broadway production. At this point, Stark and Merrick were at odds over who would have the last say on production decisions. It was a power war, and Stark was not going down without a fight. 'Life is too short to deal with Ray Stark,' Merrick stated as he walked away from the contract. For a week, Streisand was in the dark. She was nearing panic, continuously on the phone to Erlichman, wolfing ice cream and roaming the floors of the night while she worried out loud to a drowsy Elliott, refusing to talk to Diana, who kept phoning to find out if she had the job or not. The show was cancelled one day and then restarted the next. Erlichman finally called her to deliver her the good news. Stark was ready to begin production, and he and Bella Linden, Streisand's lawyer, were renegotiating better terms for her.

She hurtled forward, self-absorbed, seduced by the temptation of her name in lights on Broadway. Elliott had not received a gig offer since his return from London. She knew he was sad about it, and she knew she should spend more time and effort working out his difficulties with him, but she couldn't stop or slow down her momentum to do so. All her fantasies were about to come true if she played her cards perfectly.

Elliott was cast as the court jester in a television version of Mary Rodgers' Once Upon a Mattress, a musical based on the fairy tale The Princess and the Pea that starred Carol Burnett as the zany princess, a role she had played in the original Broadway production five years earlier. Burnett had risen to prominence as a television personality since then. Even though it was only for two weeks, it was Elliott's first job since On the Town. Streisand went without him for auditions in Boston and Philadelphia. She was given a suite at the Ritz Carlton Hotel in Boston. She understood from the start that Funny Girl was her one-way path to stardom. Everything in her was now aimed around her becoming a celebrity. That meant more responsibility, but it also meant that if she succeeded - and she refused to believe otherwise - she would not only be on her way, but she would have already arrived.

She understood from the start that Funny Girl was her one-way path to stardom. Everything in her was now aimed around her becoming a celebrity. That meant more responsibility, but it also meant that if she succeeded - and she refused to believe otherwise - she would not only be on her way, but she would have already arrived.

SWIMMING IN Streisand walked off the train in Boston, wearing a new mink coat and a matching hat pulled down over her ears. It was late afternoon on January 7, 1964, and Funny Girl would open six days later at the Shubert Theater. Carol Haney initiated new dance sequences, Irene Sharaff altered costumes, Isobel Lennart continuously rewrote the second act, and Styne and Merrill finished five new songs that would ultimately be eliminated before they departed Boston.

Funny Girl premiered in Boston on January 13th. Following the show, the cast gathered in a nearby diner to await the morning reviews. 'For some reason,' explains John Patrick, 'I was given the critics' reviews to read aloud at the table where we were all seated. When I read aloud a critic who remarked, "Miss Streisand can sing, but she certainly can't act," Streisand fell into tears and lay her head down on the table. "That's nonsense - you can act!" I told her. But I don't think she was paying attention. She nearly instantly departed the table."

Streisand, like many other recording artists who had soared to the top of the charts with startling rapidity, had no idea how wealthy she was. Accountants handled her financial matters and paid her invoices. She claims she received a weekly allowance of $25. She, on the other hand, rarely paid for anything out of her own pocket. She was high on life, but not carefree. She would never give up her passion of bargaining, an art at which she had already become an expert. A discount was expected whether she was dealing with a butcher or an antique dealer. 'Let's see, with 20% off that means -' she would begin. 'Whaddaya mean that's your price?' she'd question, disappointed if the answer was no, 'I deserve something.'

Before heading on tour, she recorded Barbra Streisand/The Third Album, which was released in February while Funny Girl was in previews in New York. A few weeks later, she finished the cast album, which was documented by a Life reporter and photographer. According to Life, she wore smudged white Capri pants, knee-high crocodile boots, a flowing, fur-collared cape, and a headpiece like a bishop's mitre. 'She was an hour late, yet she walked into the room full of irritated musicians with the assurance of Clyde Beatty. The cane chair and whip in her hand were practically visible. She didn't need to warm up, and when she sang, she was flawless.'

Within three weeks of its release - before the show premiered - the Funny Girl cast album was ranked second on Variety's list of best-selling albums. The Third Album debuted at Number Twenty-One and began to climb the chart, while The Second Album remained in the top ten. At the same time, 'People' was in the top ten on the singles list. Streisand was earning more money from her records than she could from the show. Marty Erlichman felt she was actually losing money because he could have booked her for big prices in the country's best nightclubs. She would consider it another time. Her focus was now on her role in a production that was gradually approaching zero hour, opening night, despite all of its postponements.

To add to her worries, Carol Channing's Hello, Dolly! had just premiered and was being heralded as the biggest musical smash since My Fair Lady debuted eight years before. Streisand was concerned that her own triumph would be overshadowed by Channing, who was the toast of Broadway and the darling of critics. Hello, Dolly! and Funny Girl are both period musicals featuring strikingly comparable numbers - StreisandDon't Rain on My Parade' and Channing's 'Before the Parade Passes Me By'. Both shows featured powerful, domineering women, though Dolly eventually gets her man.

The first and last scenes were still unset the day before opening night. Jerry Robbins had Fanny enter with two leashed Russian wolfhounds. Handling the dogs while crossing the stage, halting midway to shrug her shoulders, and then continuing proved more difficult than any of her flashy musical acts, thanks to the misbehaviour of the animals. The tableau stayed until the final screening, after which the dogs were dismissed, leaving Streisand frazzled. The sequence was rehearsed the next morning, with Fanny sweeping on and across the stage as before, but without the animals. The last scene was reworked and rehearsed just three hours before the curtain rose on March 26, 1964.

Streisand was overcome with worry. Elliott stayed in her dressing room until her last call. She crushed the umpteenth cigarette she had puffed on intermittently while waiting. Her dresser double-checked her costume and hair. The assistant stage manager led her across the wide backstage space to the wing from which she would enter.

The orchestra was led into the concluding notes of the overture by Milton Rosenstock. The curtain rose, and she moved forward on stage to make her appearance. There was a loud ovation when she reached mid-stage, which surprised her because she had not expected so many of her record admirers to be in the audience. After each of her solos, the ovation was deafening. Her ability to match Fanny Brice's skills for comedy and sorrow outweighed any criticisms of the weak text or the skimpiness of the Ziegfeld Follies numbers that the production's mounting costs had exacted. Her majestic descent down a Ziegfeld staircase as a pregnant bride while a tenor sang 'His Love Makes Me Beautiful' was as memorable as Channing's descent down the famed red-carpeted stairwell at the Harmonia Gardens. There were no dancing waiters to sweep her off her feet at the bottom of the staircase, but her 'Oy vey, am I pretty!' as she shamelessly marketed her condition by wrapping her arms around the bulging stomach beneath her opulent wedding gown brought the audience to its feet. It was also evident that the almost-scrapped piece, 'People,' which she performed standing alone on a stage lit by a summer moon, was the show's hit and that, whatever happened to Funny Girl, Barbra Streisand was now a bona fide star.

MAKING IT

'I always knew I wanted to be famous.

I knew it; I wanted it; I was never content.

I was always trying to be something I wasn't.

I wanted to prove to the world that they

shouldn't make fun of me.'

BARBRA STREISAND, 1966

CHAPTER 4

Streisand's affair with Sharif grew more intense while she was in New York with ELLIOTT. She had transformed into the character she was playing, madly in love with the stunning Nicky Arnstein. She had fantasised about herself as the woman in the story since she was a child, rather than the movie star who played her. 'I never aspired to be Vivien Leigh,' she stated. 'I wished I could be Scarlett O'Hara.' She thought Scarlett and Rhett were real individuals, and the love sequences in the film had the feel of cinéma vérité, with real people in genuine love. Wyler witnessed what was going on but said nothing because the rushes were fiery and just what he desired. She shone both on and off the screen. The set was buzzing with rumours - would she quit Elliott? Will Sharif divorce his wife? The couple stayed inconspicuous off the set until toward the end of filming, when they were photographed together at numerous social functions, and these sightings were published in the press. Elliott called her from New York, heartbroken and outraged, after they were seen together at an exclusive charity fashion show at the Factory Discothèque in Hollywood.

'Why in the hell did you go to the fashion show with Omar?' he yelled over the phone.

'Because the ticket would have cost me $250,' he responded, and she agreed. Elliott, unable to assume the position of the duped husband, evidently accepted that statement at face value. Furthermore, it did not seem unreasonable given that Streisand had retained many of her previous money-saving habits and was always grateful when someone picked up the tab for her. The next Sunday night, she dined with Sharif alone at Matteo's, one of Hollywood's 'in' restaurants.

'Barbra's always been a cheapskate,' Elliott told journalist Irv Kupcinet, hoping to prevent a scandal. She agreed to those dates with Sharif since she dislikes cooking for herself.' When confronted by Sheilah Graham, he stated, 'I'm furious with Barbra and told her so. She should have realised she was in a terrible situation out there, where the press disliked her for being reluctant. I'm really enraged with her for putting herself in this situation. I'm a really secure person, yet I have certain reactions as a man.'

By downplaying the relationship, he was sending a message to the public that Streisand had done nothing wrong, that she was simply horribly naive. The issue deteriorated when Sharif admitted to a Los Angeles Times reporter, 'It's true, I lusted over Barbra.'

Streisand's ego was boosted by such a passionate revelation from a lover, who was a handsome leading man known to have had affairs with some of the world's most attractive women. Critical comments about her nose and appearance were constantly appearing in print, and despite her ability to laugh at them in public, they hurt - a lot. She urgently desired to be perceived as a desirable, attractive lady, but perhaps even more so, she desired to feel that way about herself. She envisioned herself as the great love of two men: her spouse and her lover. Elliott would be expected to fly to her side and fight for her in such a case.

His reaction to the affair was not what she had expected. Elliott treated it as if it were a fabrication of the press and remained in New York. Streisand, enraged by his calm demeanour, became increasingly vocal about the value of her connection with Sharif. 'I know Elliott thinks it's just another Hollywood fantasy,' she explained to a reporter, 'but it's not - Omar has told me many times that he loves me.'

Sharif, she rapidly discovered, had his own notion of love. It was something he could collect and then put on a shelf, in his opinion. After finishing his sequences before Streisand's, he left Hollywood for Europe a few days later to feature in Mayerling alongside Catherine Deneuve, James Mason, and Ava Gardner. Within a few weeks, rumours began to circulate that he was having an affair with Ava. In this usually tawdry Hollywood love triangle, both Streisand and Elliott seemed like naive fools. When Elliott returned to California, they acted as if nothing had happened between them, at least in public. Elliott, who was already struggling with being the less successful husband of a celebrity, was severely harmed by Streisand's behaviour. Streisand, for one, was no longer certain of her feelings for Elliott.

They were still living together, but they were seeing different lawyers in an attempt to reach an amicable trial separation agreement. A press release was prepared, then yanked back, brought out again, and yanked back again. Because Elliott was a partner in both of her businesses, their common corporate interests were entangled, and Jason's custody posed issues. Elliott desired to have the child with him for an extended period of time, but Streisand refused to compromise. She intended to stay in Hollywood while Elliott was in New York, making joint custody impossible with such a young child.

This was not your typical narrative about the cost of fame. Streisand and Elliott both struggled with deep-seated emotional issues prior to their celebrity. Elliott's love and dedication had evidently not been enough to instil confidence in her as a woman. Regardless of how successful she was, she struggled with self-doubt. Winning the heart of her attractive leading man had helped, but only for a short while. She needed greater freedom to discover herself and expand her personal experiences. Still, she wasn't sure if she wanted to or should let go of Elliott. She restarted her therapy sessions. Her long-running investigation into her past and the causes of her actions, worries, and insecurities resumed. She would spend years talking about her father's death and her difficult childhood.

Between 1966 and 1970, Barbra Streisand established herself as one of the era's most varied artists. She continued to advance in her singing career by releasing the album "Color Me Barbra" in 1966. This was also the year she featured in a special television program of the same name, demonstrating her artistic talent and range.

By 1967, Streisand had not only published the album "Simply Streisand," but she had also begun shooting "Funny Girl," a project that would propel her to new heights. Fanny Brice's work not only helped her win her first Academy Award in 1968, but it also displayed her unique acting ability.

In 1969, she starred in the critically acclaimed musical film "Hello, Dolly!" During this time, Streisand was also continually producing music, which helped to expand her song repertoire.

She appeared in "The Owl and the Pussycat" in 1970, demonstrating her various acting abilities in a comic role. She also continued her music career by releasing several albums, which received widespread acclaim.

During this time, not only did Streisand's profession develop, but her personal life also changed dramatically, from being married to having children to juggling career and family life. With her unique voice and natural acting talent, she became an artistic icon, grabbing people's hearts.

During the 1970s, Barbra Streisand not only cemented her place in the entertainment world, but she also demonstrated her versatility as an artist. Streisand demonstrated that her acting abilities were not restricted to serious roles with the success of films such as "The Owl and the Pussycat" (1970) and "What's Up, Doc?" (1972). In music, the albums "Stoney End" and "Barbra Joan Streisand" emphasised her distinct voice.

The album "The Way We Were" was one of Streisand's greatest commercial triumphs between 1973 and 1974. The song of the same name became a major smash, propelling her to the pinnacle of celebrity. The film of the same name also helped her acquire a lot of attention for her acting.

Streisand's career was transformed in 1975 and 1976 when she took on the roles of director and producer for the film "A Star is Born." This film not only became a commercial triumph, but it also helped her win the Academy Award for Best Original Song. This demonstrates her talent and versatility in her profession.

Streisand continued to create albums in the closing years of the decade, including "Superman" (1977), "Songbird" (1978), and "Wet" (1979), each with a distinct sound, demonstrating Her flexibility and limitless innovation in music.

Streisand's personal life, in addition to her artistic career, experienced numerous ups and downs, including her divorce from Elliot Gould in 1971. Nonetheless, she retained her position as a mother and continued her charitable and social activities.

In short, the 1970s not only saw the steady expansion of Streisand's career, but they also saw her demonstrate her vast ability in numerous artistic domains, ranging from music to movie to producing. as well as the director.

MAKING MOVIES, MAKING LOVE

'One of the reasons I care about being a movie actress is to be remembered, to be slightly immortal; because I think life is so short that by the time we get to see things with some sense of reality and truth, it's all over. I'm sure that's why I care so much about making movies: It prolongs your life.'

BARBRA STREISAND, 1977

'People say I got this strange hold over Barbra.

I do. It's called love.'

JON PETERS, 1977

CHAPTER 5

She had taken an emotional trip back to her roots the previous year, 1979. She was never a completely practising Jew, yet she felt deeply Jewish. She had diligently researched the time, the history of the Eastern European Jews, and the laws and social structure that shaped their world in the late nineteenth and early twentieth centuries to better comprehend the culture and reasons in Yentl. She sought for experts in the topic, rabbis from the faith's three branches, Orthodox, Conservative, and Reform.1 At the same time, Jason was approaching his thirteenth birthday and preparing for his bar mitzvah. The service, which takes place in a synagogue or temple, is neither a sacrament nor a sacramental ritual. It simply marks the arrival of a Jewish kid at the age when adult reason and responsibility, supposedly, begin. It is normally celebrated on the Saturday closest to the boy's birthday, which was 5 January 1980 in Jason's instance.

Streisand and Elliott, who had been separated from Jenny at the time, had both met Rabbi Daniel Lapin of the Pacific Jewish Center. 'I explained to her,' the Rabbi remembered, 'that in order for the bar mitzvah to have any meaning, in a deeper sense, for her son, he would have to know and understand that it meant something to her, too.' Rabbi Lapin advised her to study Judaism alongside Jason. This was perfectly timed with her Yentl research. She would meet with the Rabbi once a week to discuss what she had learnt and to address difficult theological concerns.

The serious study of their faith and past drew her closer to Jason, who had grown into an educated young man with a sense of humour and a wide range of interests. He enjoyed writing, and his school essays demonstrated his talent. He seems to enjoy spending more quiet time with his mother and working on a project with her. During her seven years with Peters, they hadn't spent as much time together as either of them would have liked.

The approaching bar mitzvah also brought her into closer touch with Elliott, albeit not romantically. That had been many years ago, but there was a strong sense of family as Elliott and his father stood on the bima with Jason, as was customary, and she, in her front-row seat in the small synagogue, watched the passing of ancient tradition from father to son as Elliott and the ageing Bernard Gould read from the Torah with Jason. Because the bar mitzvah is a cheerful event, a party following the ritual is appropriate. The Malibu property was outfitted with three tents. Kosher and Chinese caterers were brought in. Streisand danced with Jason and a nimble Bernard, as well as with Elliott, who also danced with Diana. Her mother later sang 'One Kiss' on the bandstand. There was joyous Jewish, Russian, and popular music, the latter so Jason and his friends could dance, though most of the young people were too shy to do so.

With Jason's bar mitzvah behind her and her business agreements with Peters finalised, she returned to the embarrassing process of pitching Yentl, this time armed with video of the Czechoslovakian locations she wanted to use and a screenplay by Ted Allen. Warner Brothers and Columbia Pictures both declined. She went to United Artists, with a budget of $14.5 million. They stated that if she sang in the film, they might consider the project. Ted Allen believes he suggested this from the beginning since Streisand did not want to make a "Ray Stark-Herbert Ross musical." This was viewed as a viable compromise by Streisand. Yentl could be described as "a realistic fantasy... a film with music." Late hours in her living room were spent with Michel Legrand at the piano, Streisand getting up from her cross-legged posture on the floor and going over to the keyboard as an idea came to her, and the Bergmans nearby writing out lyrics to proposed songs by Legrand.

She was currently working on the screenplay with the assistance of renowned author Isaac Bashevis Singer. Ted Allen speculated that the script he created and she rejected 'had symptoms of the anti-Semitism in Eastern Europe that drove the Jews to America, and I don't think Barbra enjoyed that. She had another idea.' What she saw in the story was Yentl's passionate desire to study the Talmud2 and possibly become a talmid chacham, a learned scholar, a Talmud expert. The talmid chacham is the most revered figure in traditional Jewish life and culture, yet women were prohibited access to the Talmud and its wisdom. Yentl performed what she did because she believed that women and men should be treated equally, and that equality could only be attained through education. It was also a narrative about unrequited love, about a young woman who loses her father, her only kindred spirit in life, and how she must cope with this awful loss.

When Legrand and the Bergmans had a handful of songs that expressed Yentl's thoughts, Streisand recorded them on tape and tried again to entice the studios. This time, United Artists stepped forward. A picture with Streisand singing was a different story, but they worked hard to negotiate a pact that would protect them if Streisand the filmmaker failed. They asked her to grant them the authority to approve the final cut. Streisand fought to maintain her dominance.

Sue Mengers gave her a significant offer while these negotiations were ongoing. Mengers was married to Belgian director Jean-Claude Tramont, who had fired Gene Hackman's co-star Lisa Eichhorn, an intelligent American-born actress who had attended London's Royal Academy of Dramatic Arts, four weeks into production on the picture All Night Long for MCA/Universal. Cheryl Gibbons, the mistreated wife who discovers her sexuality with the night-manager of an Ultra-Save Drugstore, an institution with an unusual clientele, required an earthiness that Eichhorn lacked in the rushes. Mengers urged Streisand to replace the fired actress after production was suspended.

The movie was really about Hackman's character, George Dopler, who hates his job, is in an unhappy marriage, and falls in love with a married woman (Gibbons) who is having an affair with his son, who wants to create Country and Western music. Cheryl Gibbons had just five or six sequences at first, but the opportunity to expand herself and play a Marilyn Monroe-style waiflike blonde temptress appealed to Streisand. The $4 million fee plus 15% of the gross that she was offered was an additional inducement. For this stipend - the largest paid to an actress in Hollywood at the time - she would only have to take six weeks off from working on the screenplay for Yentl, and the money would help her finance the picture.

After a four-week hiatus while her role was being developed, production on All Night Long resumed on June 9, 1980, and remained on location in and around Los Angeles for the next six weeks, despite a heatwave and, in the final week, a major strike by the Screen Actors Guild involving residuals on video, cable, and pay television. Streisand only had one more scene to film, in which she would slide down a fire pole (her spouse in the film was a fireman). She didn't return to finish the last shot until late October, after the strike had ended. 'Uh-uh,' she murmured, horrified as she stood on the edge of the second-floor perch where she was to hold the pole for her descent, 'I don't think I can do it. I have a sensitive stomach.' She executed the slide in one take after numerous members of the team and Hackman himself slid down it to prove to her that she would be fine.

All Night Long was not a hit with Barbra Streisand fans. She performed her blowsy, sexually awakened housewife exactly on note, in character, with no razzle-dazzle or Streisand characteristics, and she backed Hackman up in some of his greatest scenes. Although it is not for everyone, the gritty American working-class reality it depicts (as seen through Tramont's unusual foreign perspective) is fascinating, Hackman offers a memorable, moving performance, and Streisand demonstrates how talented she is as an actress. But all of her attention was now focused on Yentl.

'I continuously had to give up everything,' Streisand said of her interactions with United Artists on Yentl. 'I didn't get paid for writing, but I did get paid on the Directors' Guild wage for directing, which I believe is around $80,000, and I got paid significantly less [$1 million] as an actress than I did in All Night Long. If we went over budget [now $16.5 million], I had to give back half my compensation. It didn't matter to me, though. Nothing was more important to me than getting this movie completed.'

There had been multiple rewrites of the screenplay by this point, including Singer's, one by Elaine May, and several by Streisand. Finally, Jule Styne chose English television writer Jack Rosenthal, creator of The Bar-Mitzvah Boy, which he had turned into an unsuccessful musical. Rosenthal and Streisand collaborated. Rosenthal repeatedly tried to eliminate Streisand's several songs, primarily ballads that seemed to break the flow of the plot, unaware that the film's finance was heavily reliant on her soundtrack CD.

They had 'huge rows' about it, but Streisand always prevailed in the end.

Yentl had taken her on a long journey, and throughout this adventure she had been forced to confront many of her demons - her sense of abandonment, of being a woman in a man's world, of viewing herself as ugly, and shame at not being the daughter she thought Diana would have liked. 'I've spent so many years feeling guilty,' she confessed. 'There is Jewish guilt. And I'm learning about life by talking to individuals and listening to what they feel and think. They have the same mishigas as me... People are terrified of their own emotions. Their sexual orientation. I had an anxiety episode the other day while driving to my [group therapy appointment]. I couldn't take a breath. I was enraged, miserable, and upset, and I thought I was going nuts. 'Like, maybe I'm insane, I'm such a bad person, and maybe I truly am these horrible things you read about, and how do I deal with it and live with myself?'But when I arrived to the session, the therapist replied, "Look, you're all insane, and so am I; the only difference is that I respect yours." He took away half of my anxiousness. Because it was OK to be insane, because we're all insane, and if you can respect your own madness - far out.'

Her 'craziness' expressed itself in her passion for things that were important to her. She was in a perpetual state of upheaval. She wore people down, wanting to instil in them her feeling of impending doom, and Yentl had become her raison d'être. Despite being compelled by United Artists to relinquish authority over the final cut, she remained steadfast in her quest to retain control over the important aspects of the film.

She had won the battle to film Yentl in Czechoslovakia and at Lee International Studios in London, where she arrived in February 1982, two months before primary photography began. One key issue remained unaddressed with United Artists. Her original contract did not require her to provide a completion bond, which is a type of Hollywood insurance in which a private business commits to pay an amount in excess of the producer's budget for the film.

'The day before we were supposed to start shooting, United Artists threatened they would shut down the project if I didn't give in and take on the completion bond,' she recounted. It was absurd because they paid the firm $700,000, which I needed to make the film [which meant she would have to make up the difference with private finances or raise it elsewhere]. They didn't believe me. 'Not in that sense, I suppose.'I prayed to my father the night before the first scene was shot. "Tell me what to do." I had no idea what to do. I had the impression that I wielded much too much power. You crave it for so long, and then you want to give it away.' In reality, she did not maintain the desired level of control. There had been the final cut, which she had been forced to sacrifice, and she had sorely wanted to engage the excellent Italian cinematographer Vittorio Storaro (Reds), but she couldn't because his $250,000 charge exceeded United Artists' budget.

'I had to tell Storaro that I couldn't afford him, and three days later I awoke in my lunacy... I had recently given away $500,000 to establish a chair in my father's name for cardiovascular research at UCLA. I was thinking to myself, "I just gave away $500,000 but I didn't treat myself to a $250,000 gift from Storaro?" It taught me a lesson about my own lack of self-esteem. And Yentl is all about it as well. Yentl, too, learns to respect herself.'

Streisand walked nervously onto the sound stage where she would shoot Yentl's opening shot on 14 April 1982, just ten days shy of her fortieth birthday. The cast and staff applauded, and she was given a director's chair with her name on it. She went around shaking hands with everyone. The sweaty palms of a prop man embarrassed him. 'Believe me, no one is more nervous than I am. We'll all make mistakes, particularly myself. I'll make the majority of them. So I need you,' she explained.

Her longtime buddy William Wyler died not long before filming began. 'You never got an opportunity to chat to Willie about Yentl,' his wife Tally wrote. But I'm sure there were things he wanted to tell you. So, if you're on the set and don't know what to do, just remain really quiet and maybe you'll hear Willie whisper in your ear.' Streisand would frequently stroll over to one side and appear to be silently communicating with Willie or her father.

Her desire to get things perfect prompted her to expect the cast and crew to do their homework. She had given a seven-volume set of books called The Legends of the Jews to Mandy Patinkin, who was playing Avigdor, the man Yentl loves but to whom she can't reveal her true identity, and several books on keeping a kosher kitchen to Amy Irving, who was cast as Hadass, the young woman Avigdor loves but who marries Yentl disguised as a boy, just prior to production.

'Barbra would try to visit as many Hasidic weddings as she could possibly find to acquire the feel of the music, movement, and crowds, and also because of the wedding scene in the film,' Jeanette Kupferman, the film's historical consultant, recalled. "Can you help me find a wedding?" became a common request... Needless to say, Barbra was a big hit with the magnificently dressed Hasidic matrons, who were blown away by her interest in them... "Is that really a sheitel?" she'd ask, one finger tucked under the elastic of a gorgeous upswept coiffure. "You must give me your wig-maker's name," ? "Say, could you tell me about Havdalah candles?" '

She claimed she got sick on her way to work every day since it was all too much for her. 'I kept thinking about what a friend of mine, Irvin Kershner, said: "One day at a time." I'm not sure how I accomplished it, but I'm glad I did. I didn't believe I'd be able to do it at times.'

The English tabloids reported she was experiencing problems with her cast and crew, who despised her haughty and dictatorial management style. To refute these charges, the crew submitted a letter to the press, signed by everyone involved, calling the accusations false. 'She has captured us all with her dedicated professionalism,' according to the letter.

'She'd adjust my hair ribbons, brush an eyelash off my cheek, and paint my lips to match the fruit on the table. Amy Irving, barely five feet four, said, 'I was like her tiny doll that she could dress up in,' her physical delicacy underlined by the gauntness of her face and the dramatic contrast of her pale skin, vivid blue eyes, and dark hair. 'She'd stand behind the camera twisting the strings of an imagined

Hadass doll, making it burp and cry until I'd completely crack up,' Irving explained.

The most difficult sequence in the film, Hadass' kiss during her seduction of Anshel/Yentl, was shot in one take. 'I had urged Amy to act extremely maidenly before that part, and she executed it magnificently,' Streisand revealed. But then, in the bedroom, when she comes on erotically, I asked her to let all her sensuality out, and she did.'

The cast and crew of Yentl, led by Streisand, departed London in early July for Prague, from whence they would go to the little village of Roztyly, a two-and-a-half hour journey away, to begin filming on the first outdoor sequences in Czechoslovakia. Heavy rains had flooded the small community, turning all of the roads into mud rivers. Despite the unusual weather, Roy Walker, the production designer, and the Czech crew who had joined the business were able to create Yentl's settlement of Yanev out of a piece that had previously been a few wooden cottages and a pig farm. Sewerage and urine odours dominated the region, and there were flies the size of beetles.

Since the democratically minded Alexander Dubek was ousted as party chief in 1970, the Soviet-dominated country, formerly famous for its experimental theatre work and numerous great films, has been in a period of heavy-booted persecution. Conditions have deteriorated twelve years later. Dissent was suppressed through a variety of means, including mass arrests, union purges, and religious persecution. However, Czechoslovakia's economy was in critical trouble, and the Czechs had been courting Western film firms looking for old-world locations for their movies, offering lower production costs and the use of the Prague film studio.

Diana was half-crazy about her daughter shooting a film in an insecure country behind the Iron Curtain, where people were being murdered or just vanished. Then there was the lack of nutritious food and the distance from home - or even from a Western hospital if something went wrong. 'She was a typical mother sobbing over the phone,' Streisand said, with a great sense of pride in her voice, adding, 'She didn't want me to go; she was afraid.' Diana cared a lot about the fact that she might be in danger. She needed to be reassured of her mother's love more than she needed to be reassured of her father's love.

She flew in veggies and fruit, two products in low supply, to ensure her company's survival. She had no idea what awaited her till she landed at Roztyly. A modest hotel across from an unappealing square was taken over by her to provide rooms for the cast and key people in the company. Members from the Czech Republic stayed with local families. Her room was unappealing: a bed against the wall, a little table with one chair in the middle, a table with a mirror next to the bed, and a damaged washbasin. Threadbare curtains covered the windows that looked out on some run-down buildings, but in the distance there were gardens full of flowers and large poplars, firs, woodlands, and a river with a bridge built during Yentl's reign.

She'd never made a picture outside of a studio's embracing paternalism, a controlled environment where she knew everything would be weighted to her benefit. She dug in, her nails stubby-short, a huge sacrifice on her part, and was never heard complaining about the conditions. The scenes in which she was both actress and director were the hardest for her to shoot. She had to figure out how to get the most out of her teammates and whether the camera was positioned correctly to fracture her concentration without losing it so she was aware of what was going on around her.

'I had to make all the decisions,' she explained, her voice filled with admiration at her own accomplishments. 'I had a co-producer who handled the day-to-day budget stuff, but I had to make all the other decisions - where we shot, how long we stayed in one spot,' says the director. Her goal was to create a realistic fantasy for Yentl. 'You make it a fantasy just by having the music,' she explained. 'Music does not exist. People do not cease singing... Yentl had lovely visuals, like fairy-tale imagery. I wanted it to be a love story.

Making Yentl, and the sixteen years she had spent working on it, had had a huge impact on her life. She was hardly a 'born-again Jew,' but she had immersed herself in her Jewishness. 'I talked to every rabbi I could find, looking for alternative perspectives from Reform, Conservative, and Orthodox rabbis. It's a complicated situation.

Through the centuries, men have discovered a method to utilise Jewish law to oppress women. That was a fascinating discovery for me. Part of me, my entire life, has always been intensely fascinated about information... I am fascinated by knowledge... By the end of the film, Yentl realises that if you truly care about yourself, you don't settle. You go on to discover more about your dreams and what you want out of life.'

Jon Peters returned to Hollywood with a fresh perspective on Yentl. He never thought Yentl was a movie Streisand should make. He is now completely behind her. She appreciated his help, but it made little difference between them. 'Yentl was Barbra's way of praying for her own father,' he explained. 'She made him up on film so she could adore him and say goodbye to him. In the film, she buried her father and dedicated it to him. When I viewed the movie, I burst into tears. Actually, I sobbed. 'I wish I had done it,' he admitted later.

That would have been a huge blunder. Yentl is distinctly Streisand's film, and it is a personal triumph until the final half-hour. Her acting is flawless, and the musical soliloquies work nicely. The image has a lyrical quality to it. She is sixteen in this film, but she was never young in A Star Is Born. She accomplished her goal of creating a romantic fantasy. It is also a film on male and female human freedom. It fails in the final section - Yentl/Anshel's marriage to Hadass after the disastrous wedding night simply does not ring true, and the final song - when Yentl is on board ship for the United States - breaks the spell that has been so marvellously cast, because the viewer is suddenly confronted with exactly the kind of musical number Streisand said she wanted to avoid.

The film Yentl premiered on November 16, 1983, in the Cinerama Dome in Hollywood. 'I raced out and got as many chocolate-covered marzipan and walnut biscuits as I could carry and sat there stuffing myself,' she admitted. 'That's how terrified I was.' She was yearning for her child to be welcomed, and the early trade reviews gave her hope.

'To say it succinctly and simultaneously, Barbra Streisand's Yentl is a triumph - a personal triumph for Streisand as producer, director, co-author, and performer, but also a magnificent work of filmmaking,' praised the Hollywood Reporter. 'At long last... she has achieved her goal. Magnificently.'

It had cost her a lot of money, and unlike the lyrics from an old Fanny Brice song, there was one thing she didn't have: her guy. Jon Peters had begun a new relationship. Jason was almost seventeen years old and set to travel to New York to attend the New York University Film School, which he had selected over the equally superb film school at the University of Southern California. Sure, he wanted to be involved in some area of film - acting, writing, directing - but he also wanted to be his own person, to put some distance between himself and his mother. She had given up valuable time at his expense to create Yentl. There was no new man in her life, at least not one who cared, and no new endeavour that had energised her.

She spent Thanksgiving with the Bergmans and returned home alone to Carolwood Drive. She no longer spent much time at the Barn. 'She denies being unhappy,' Elliott added. 'But she's really depressed. She doesn't have a life - at least not a true one - and it's unclear whether she'll ever be capable of loving.'

She vehemently denied it, but she had spent much of her life loving a phantom father. And what chance did Elliott, Jon, or any other guy have against a perfected by a bereaved daughter's dreams? Wasn't she, like Yentl, suddenly free? She remained optimistic that the right man would come into her life. She had resumed her contact with the married man she had been seeing before meeting Jon, but his position had not changed. She would focus on finding another narrative that captured her heart. In the meanwhile, she would return to treatment.

She met Richard Baskin, the heir to the Baskin-Robbins ice cream company, at a small Christmas social gathering and they were both attracted to each other. A bear-like man over six feet four inches tall, his intimidating bulk, Samson-like dark curly hair, and protective demeanour drew out the deeply feminine woman within her, and her fragility was met with a soft place in him. He'd seen Yentl and told her how great it was, how much its ethnic roots had moved him. He played the guitar, wrote lyrics, and was the musical director on

Honeysuckle Rose, a low-key film starring Willie Nelson about a Country music star. His had been a privileged childhood and youth, similar to Barry Dennen. He went into the Carolwood Drive house in February, a decade younger than Streisand, a self-contained, cerebral man who was pleased to become her boyfriend - which he soon became. Friends speculated that it was a Streisand whim. It wouldn't last long. Where had the smashing cymbals and dramatic moments gone in her significant love affairs? She'd grow tired of compatibility and prefer a more stimulating confrontational connection. They were still dating two years later.

CHAPTER 6

'She should only live and be happy,' Diana told a neighbour who was critical of Streisand's live-in relationship with the much younger Baskin. The old scars would not heal, but Diana appeared to have softened, to have grown less critical. Roslyn, who had moved out of her mother's apartment but remained in Los Angeles, was struggling in her work. She had a lovely voice and was pretty, but she lacked Streisand's drive and extraordinary talent. The half-sisters' relationship was complicated, with rivalries, resentments, and jealousies that had yet to be resolved. Roslyn had expected Streisand to assist her in her pursuit of a career in film. She had non-speaking extra parts in two of her sister's films: A Star Is Born, where she sits at Streisand's table during the Grammy Awards scene, and The Main Event, where she is one of the women working out in the aerobics class with Streisand at the start of the film. Streisand couldn't think of anything else she could or should do for Roslyn. But the feelings of guilt lingered.

'Everyone wants a small bit of me,' she grumbled to a close friend. 'I have to be cautious.' She was concerned about Jason. He appeared to be struggling to discover himself, and they could not communicate effectively. Telephone discussions were unsatisfying, and when he returned home for the holidays, she seemed to be immersed in a time-consuming work assignment. Baskin stayed in the house, but acquaintances saw a change in their relationship. There was evidence of backbiting and a disintegrating romanticism where there had once been harmony. "Can't you stop working at seven o'clock?" all the guys in my life have said. 'I had no idea what they meant,' she told an interviewer.

Work took over her life, and she was repeating herself--bringing the man from her romantic life into her work, putting him in a position of power but forcing him to deal with her as the ultimate authority, and setting a standard that he felt he had to live up to or his masculinity would be compromised. Baskin was knowledgeable in music and recording procedures, so she collaborated with him in that aspect of her profession.

With no film projects on the horizon in the late summer of 1985, she decided to return to her roots and record an album of Broadway tunes. 'It's about time I accomplished something important,' she told New York Times music critic Stephen Holden.

She felt she had to quit recording songs 'that any number of other people could sing as well as, if not better than she could. She wished to do something in which she truly believed. 'Broadway music is the music I adore; it's where I came from; it's where my origins are,' she said. Despite having recorded scores of songs with rock rhythm sections, she felt out of her element singing music with a strong, consistent backbeat... Because I am a vocalist who believes in the moment. Each take of a song is unique to me. You can't do that with rock and roll because everyone says you have to sing to the beat, which is extremely difficult for me.'

She re-joined forces with Marty Erlichman, with whom she had separated during the Jon Peters years because Peters had effectively served as her manager. Erlichman approached Columbia Records about doing a Broadway album. 'Barbra's contract with them states she needs to deliver X albums, but they have to be authorised records, which means most of them have to be modern,' he stated. This record would not be approved by Columbia. It was not regarded as a pop album. As a result, she didn't get the advance she was due, and it wouldn't count as an approved record deal unless it sold 2.5 million copies, at which point it would automatically become an approved album, whether they approved it in advance or not.'

She pushed on with her plans despite her belief that Broadway songs were no longer popular. Under pressure from the record label, she agreed to a single slip LP instead of a double record. She called Peter Matz, with whom she had not worked in a long time, and asked him if he would accept to co-produce, arrange, and lead the orchestra. Matz, who orchestrated the majority of her early albums and was undoubtedly responsible for their success, concurred. They would write and record the majority of the tracks. Baskin and David Foster would be in charge of production for the other selections.1 The four of them began marathon listening sessions to locate a blend of rare music and standards' (Streisand was quickly and completely immersed).

After weeks of listening to show scores by Kern, Hammerstein, Rodgers and Hart, Bernstein, Berlin, the Gershwins, and other renowned Broadway composers, she focused on Stephen Sondheim, a composer she had mostly disregarded during her early recording and concert career. 'It's like growing into a Medea or Hedda Gabler role,' she remarked. 'It's bad when you're twenty. You should be older.' She had recorded Sondheim's 'There Won't Be Trumpets' from Anyone Can Whistle for an unreleased cut from the Butterfly album in 1974, but then changed her mind since Columbia wanted her to do more modern songs with simpler lyrics. She was intrigued by Sondheim's elegance and intellectualism now that she recognized their complexity.

'Putting It Together,' from Sondheim's then-current musical, the Pulitzer Prize-winning Sunday in the Park with George, piqued her interest. Despite the fact that they had never met, she called him at his home in New York. 'I informed him about my talk with my record label... about my desire to record an album of Broadway songs. And they were quite reluctant and dissatisfied, saying, "Barbra, you can't do a record like this." It's not for profit. This is similar to your old records. Nobody is going to believe it." Every word they said simply boosted my confidence. I wanted to incorporate all of their suggestions into this song. And I thought, "What a great way to open this album."

The original lyrics of the song were about the art world, as the primary character in the musical was the French painter George Seurat. 'She wanted to make [the song] relevant to the music business, so she asked me if she could modify one word to replace "lasers," and I suggested, "Why not use 'vinyl' instead?" Sondheim recalled. and she jumped at it, thinking it was fantastic. "Let me look at the rest of the lyrics if you want to personalise it," I said. I'm confident I can make it more record-oriented and less art-related," as it was in the context of the exhibition. It becomes enjoyable to do once you get into it, which is why I did it.'

'I could chat to him for hours,' continued Streisand. 'I felt I couldn't deny the truth... you don't hide it; you use it,' she says. "Here I am, a very successful recording star, and yet I have to fight for everything I believe in," I told him. I've been auditioning for twenty-three years." When I asked him if he could incorporate that idea, he penned, "Even though you get the recognition/Everything you do you still audition." 'Do you understand what I mean?'

Sondheim had never been known to write a song just for a singer. 'Barbra Streisand has one of the two or three best singing voices in the world,' he said. 'It's not just her voice, but also her energy, passion, and command. She possesses the painstaking attention to detail that distinguishes a skilled artist... Although every detail has been considered, you cannot see all of the effort and decisions that went into the labour. It's as if she just got out of the shower and started singing at you.'

'He thinks, as I do, that art is a living process, that it's not fixed in stone, that it breathes and evolves and changes,' Streisand adds of Sondheim. It blew my mind when I told him, "I never understood 'Send in the Clowns.'" What do you think about writing a second bridge to explain more about this relationship?" And no worries. I've asked him to make numerous modifications like that, and at first, we'd be on the phone, and he'd say, "Wait a minute. That is not possible." Then he says, "Let me call you back," and two hours later he phones me back, and it's all done. I'm not sure how he does these things. He's extremely well-organised.'

The Broadway Album became a predominantly Streisand-sings-Sondheim album as she added to 'Putting It Together', 'Send in the Clowns' (A Little Night Music), 'Somewhere' and 'Something's Coming' (West Side Story, music by Bernstein), 'Not While I'm Around' and 'Pretty Woman' (Sweeney Todd), and 'The Ladies Who Lunch' and 'Being Alive' (Company).

Working with Sondheim was 'one of the most thrilling partnerships I've ever had, because we both communicate fast, think fast; so it was like shorthand half the time... we literally didn't have to finish sentences,' she says. It was so exciting that I was screaming with joy over the phone at times.'

Sondheim visited the Coast and collaborated with her on the recording sessions. Here were two of music's genuinely towering talents, both strong personalities and perfectionists. Sondheim, dressed in a sweatshirt and sneakers, would pluck at his close-cropped pepper and salt beard as he laboured over each syllable he scrawled out on a pad of music paper, sitting on one chair, his feet up on another. Streisand, dressed casually in a running suit, waited uneasily nearby. She regarded Sondheim as one of the twentieth century's greatest theatre composers. His mind was as rapid as hers, and he had an instinctual understanding of how to tailor his words and music to her specific demands.

'Everyone in the studio understood they were a part of something momentous,' said Alan Bergman, who attended the majority of the three-week session with Marilyn. Rather than fleeing to the halls, the musicians sat in their chairs and listened to the playbacks. Every try was unique - a new meaning for a sentence, a new twist on a note.'

The album was published in early November 1985 and quickly rose to the top of the Billboard list (an incredible 800,000 advance sales). Streisand had always believed in it, but she had not expected it to be such a huge success, and it restored her faith in the public's appreciation for fine music. She was convinced that if she followed her gut about what was best for her, she would succeed, and she had shown this once more.

'The Broadway Album sparkles with full-bodied, sensitive bel canto versions of ballads by Stephen Sondheim, Rodgers and Hammerstein, and a Porgy and Bess medley that rank among the most electrifying performances of [Streisand's] 23-year career,' New York Times critic Stephen Holden observed.

The same drive that drove her to take on a film adaptation of Tom Topor's play, Nuts, about a high-class prostitute who kills one of her clients in self-defence, drove her to take on a film adaptation of Tom Topor's play, Nuts. Further, it posed the question, 'What is normal?' Several writers tried and failed to develop a script that would delight her. Finally, she remembered two of them, Darryl Ponicsan and Alvin Sargent, who were working on a script at the time. While she awaited the outcome of their work, she saw Richard Dreyfuss in the

Los Angeles Company's production of Larry Kramer's The Normal Heart, convinced that she had acquired a new vision for herself. The wheelchair-bound Dr Brookner (a role she would grow and expand) captivated both her brain and her emotions, and she was confident she could portray it not just well, but with genuine understanding.

She thought the play was about everyone having the right to love, which she thought had international appeal. It was also about the alarming absence of government aid in developing a cure for AIDS, and she wanted to do something constructive to bring the world's attention to the disease's heinous devastation. The two weeks she'd spent with Kramer in their tight, passionate, violent story meetings in the Carolwood Drive house's study had convinced her that The Normal Heart could be one of the most important films she'd ever produce.

They chatted for hours about homosexuality, mothers and sons, AIDS, and how the narrative should be conveyed more from Dr Brookner's perspective as an AIDS specialist. They focused on her frustration, her fight for greater research funding, and the bond she had with Ned, the play's lead character, a gay activist similar to Kramer.

'I felt immense warmth toward her,' Kramer adds, his piercing brown eyes fixed on a recollection. 'I left thinking we were in accord.' He expected he would be in charge of the final screenplay for The Normal Heart, which was semi-autobiographical and a raw portrayal of his life. When he returned to New York, his lawyer informed him that Streisand was requesting the right to hire another writer on the script if she believed it was necessary. She was adamant about it. She had to have the last say over the script. Kramer, who had his own production business and produced and adapted for the cinema D.H. Lawrence's Women in Love (1969), for which he was nominated for an Academy Award, refused to give in to this demand, and the transaction fell through.

Streisand was devastated. Losing the rights was a huge loss for her, but she refused to give up hope that she would one day make The Normal Heart, a conviction reinforced by the AIDS deaths of many of her former close associates, including Liberace. She realised she couldn't give up what she regarded as her vision, the only thing she truly trusted, and she couldn't produce and direct a picture if she didn't have complete control over the script. Some may see this as a desire for power. It went even deeper. Making a film in which she was so deeply immersed meant risking her life and her ability to produce art that would last. 'It's like a line from Steve Sondheim's "Finishing the Hat,"' she says. 'See, I made a hat when there was never a hat.'

She was once again passionately interested in her first love, filmmaking, and it was a world in which Richard Baskin, as he had suddenly appeared to be in her home, was an alien. She had surrounded herself with female colleagues, which made her feel more at ease and better able to relate to women. With her secretary Kim Skalecki staying in the guest house and a staff of female aides on the premises every day, she was rarely alone, and work continued into the evening hours. She also had to make time for the management of her vast business empires, the supervision of the Barbra Streisand Foundation - which distributed over $1 million yearly to various causes ranging from AIDS to abused children, battered women, university medical chairs (in her father's name), environmental and civil rights groups, and supplying musical instruments to lower grade schools so that the young students could play in a band - and, on top of all of that, her pre-presidential campaign. Her relationship with Baskin, while not as intense (or as passionate) as her romance with Peters, was under great strain. Then came the disastrous Chernobyl nuclear power plant catastrophe, which pushed her back into two more circles of activity that she had avoided for nearly a decade: live concerts and politics.

'April 26th, 1986,' Marilyn Bergman recalled. '(Barbra and I) were discussing the Chernobyl disaster. She called me that morning, completely shocked by what had occurred. "What can be done about this?" was the inquiry. And he responded by saying, "The only thing that I know to do about it is to take back the Senate for the Democrats." '

Bergman was a founding member of the Hollywood Women's Political Committee, which was created two years earlier in response to widespread anti-Reagan fervour. HWPC intended to influence the vote by raising enormous quantities of campaign money for their preferred candidates through gala dinners and balls, and worked 'on the clear assumption that politicians might learn from listening to their Hollywood contributors'. The film business had proven to be an invaluable campaign supporter. There were six Democratic senate candidates in close races at the time of the Chernobyl accident.

Streisand was not a member of HWPC, but she would soon become one. Bergman suggested she perform a performance to help raise funds for the Democratic anti-nuclear candidates. Streisand felt apprehensive. 'I'm still not comfortable singing in front of a large audience in public,' she countered.

'It became a debate about which was scarier: playing in front of an audience or nuclear devastation,' Bergman remarked.

The months that followed could be dubbed "Barbra Streisand's political awakening." Bergman had lunch with Stanley Sheinbaum, an avid liberal activist, a few days after her conversation with Streisand, and told him that her friend wanted to learn more about nuclear issues. Sheinbaum agreed to take up the assignment. Dinners were set up at his house and on Carolwood Drive so she could meet with policy experts who would brief her on the subject. Leading scientists such as Marvin L. Goldberger, then President of the California Institute of Technology, and Stanford's Sidney Drell were recruited to serve as tutors.

Sheinbaum presented Streisand with nuclear policy literature, books, and essays throughout the Reagan administration. She was a dedicated student. 'She began with very little information and a great deal of abruptly awakened anxiety,' Goldberger recounted. I had two roles: one as someone who knows a lot about nuclear power and reactors, and the other as someone who has spent a lot of time worrying about strategic weapons and international security. So, in a way, I was a resource person who tried to differentiate fact from fiction for her when appropriate. Second, both I and my wife considered what vehicle would best enable her to make the greatest possible contribution in this area about which she was really concerned.'

From there, Marilyn Bergman took over. 'Marilyn realised that the only way Barbra Streisand could assist the Democrats reclaim the Senate was to raise money,' HWPC treasurer attorney Bonnie Reiss explained, 'and the only way she could do that was to perform.'

Streisand was resistant to change. Her anxiety had grown since she had missed so many concerts over the years. Finally, in mid-summer, with the election just three months away, she agreed to conduct a concert, but it would have to be limited to invited visitors and held at her remote, well-protected Malibu estate. Tents were to be erected over formal outdoor dining tables. The logistical feat of carving out an amphitheatre from a stretch of flat lawn and wiring it for sound and lights in three weeks was required to transform the ranch grounds into a professional outdoor auditorium. Regardless, everyone at the HWPC was excited because not only would Streisand be performing live for the first time in many years, but she would be doing it in her own house, a huge draw for potential ticket purchasers who were being asked to pay $5,000 to see the event.

No one was more ecstatic about the event than Barbra Streisand. 'Despite my protests that I didn't want to sing in public anymore,' she added. 'Lethal radiation had erupted from Chernobyl. The arms race was bankrupting both the United States and the world. And I wanted to add my voice to the chorus of demands for action.' The dinner-concert was called One Voice, and it had a twofold meaning: it was a solo show (though Barry Gibb sang two songs with her) and it conveyed the idea that everyone can make a difference in the battle against nuclear energy proliferation. Baskin collaborated with her as musical producer, Randy Kerber was the musical director, Streisand and Marty Erlichman were executive producers, and Gary Smith and Dwight Hennion, who had presented most of her television shows, were to produce the live concert for Home Box Office, with proceeds going to the Barbra Streisand Foundation.

Despite the pressing demands of her work on Nuts, which was nearing completion, Streisand oversaw the transformation of her property into a professional outdoor arena, co-wrote the script with Marilyn and Alan Bergman, prepared and rehearsed seventeen songs, and recorded hundreds of individual, personalised invitations on audio cassette, 'which,' one observer wrote, 'landed on the decks of Hollywood's most powerful men and women like a summons'. Over 300 persons, the capacity crowd, put in their cheques within a few days.

Streisand was flushed with nervous excitement as she waited for her entrance music in the newly created, temporary dressing-room area behind the stage on the night of the concert, September 6, 1986, a warm evening tempered by a mild Pacific wind. Robin Williams, clearly taken aback by the star-studded audience, began the show with some amusing banter. Some of Hollywood's greatest stars (and liberal Democrats) sat on impeccable white chairs set up in semi-circular rows on the grass skirt facing the stage, including Shirley MacLaine, Warren Beatty, Sally Field, Bette Midler, Jane Fonda, Goldie Hawn, Walter Matthau, Jack Nicholson, and Chevy Chase, among others, and in a grand show of solidarity, ex-husband Elliott Gould, ex-lover Jon Peters, and Jason. Streisand would be assessed by her peers, but they were also her friends, individuals who shared her political beliefs. They were all here to support a cause they all believed in, so she knew she'd have a receptive audience, not that she'd ever offer anything less than her all.

Her arrival, dressed in a flattering white beaded turtleneck sweater and a white evening skirt cut to the knee, was received with loud ovation. 'You're a nice person. You're all buddies. 'Thank you for coming,' she said, smiling and waving and kissing. The star-lit sky provided refuge. A gentle breeze blew wisps of her frizzy blonde hair, which she wore free and to her shoulders. Rather than the customary thirty-five-man orchestra, she had enlisted a flexible bunch of largely synthesiser instrumentalists - 'Eight guys and some enormous electric bill!' she exclaimed to her audience. Randy Kerber took the lead from behind the keyboards.

Her songs were tailored to the evening's theme - saving and protecting the environment, our love for others, our pride in our country - giving the concert a soft, often sentimental edge, though there were some satirical jabs at Republicans in specially written lyrics by the Bergmans. She made a lovely transition from a short lecture about nuclear energy non-proliferation to 'People,' performed with more wisdom than enthusiasm and adding fresh meaning to the lyrics. 'Over the Rainbow,' she declared, was "the greatest movie song ever written." It was dedicated to Judy Garland, who was so associated with it. As a song of enormous promise, Streisand sang it against an excellent piano background by Kerber. The bridge looked exceptionally young and carefree. She could easily have been Dorothy on the way to Oz, a young girl filled with wonder and still holding on to her fantasies. Garland's underlying request for affection and protection, as well as her fragile voice and tearful eyes, which had reflected serious human pain, were smothered. Streisand had transformed the song into her own, and it was a triumph. She even enhanced Yip Harburg's slightly syrupy ending by changing it from 'if cheerful little bluebirds fly' to the more general 'if all those little bluebirds fly'.

The two duets with Barry Gibb, 'Highway to the Sky' and 'Who's Sorry Now?,' were the evening's least successful. Then came an extremely touching rendition of Yentl's score's 'Papa Can You Hear Me?' sung as night fell, in the flickering light of a single candle: 'in commemoration of all those great father figures - Abraham Lincoln, John F. Kennedy, Gandhi, Sadat'. This was followed by 'The Way We Were,' which featured a far more modern feel than any prior arrangement, as well as multiple melismatic parts. She closed the evening with a passionate rendition of 'America the Beautiful,' beginning acappella and then inviting the audience to join in. They linked hands and swung as if moved by the night breeze.

Streisand was visibly moved by the outpouring of emotion from her audience. Her eyes welled up with tears as she exited the stage following her final bow. She missed the rapid thrill and outpouring of love she received from a live audience, as much as she had grown to fear public engagements.

The earnings from the dinner-concert exceeded by $500,000 the proceeds from a Republican fund-raising dinner for President Reagan the following night, causing tremendous happiness among HWPC members and a sense of pride in Streisand. There was no doubt that the big sum raised by Streisand's concert helped Democrats reclaim the Senate, as five of the six senators who received campaign donations from the event were elected.

With the concert, Streisand became an active member of the HWPC, which was primarily comprised of women "rising steadily through the Hollywood power structure, to establish themselves as forces within the industry." Her political consciousness had fully awakened (her social consciousness had always been present), and there would be no turning back. She would be candid and straight forward in speaking out for what she believed in and supported from this point forward, so much so that there were frequent unsubstantiated rumours that she planned to run for the Senate.

Streisand was jolted awake at 7:42 a.m. on October 1 by a powerful earthquake that struck California and measured 6.1 on the Richter scale. It claimed six lives and sent over 100 people to the hospital. Homes were seriously damaged, and cars were crushed beneath the falling concrete. It had struck with tremendous force. She rang Diana right away to make sure she was okay, and once that was confirmed, she investigated the house for damage, which turned out to be modest. But she was left worrying about when the 'big one' would strike. Aside from that, the earthquake seemed to represent the abrupt changes in her life.

Her relationship with Richard Baskin ended, and he left the Carolwood Drive house. 'He was there one day and gone the next,' a buddy observed. 'I was taken aback. She genuinely likes him.' His leaving should have been more devastating, given that they had lived together for three years. The main reason could have been that she had been off-screen for the majority of that time. Making movies, her favourite hobby, had always resulted in emotional encounters between her and the important men in her life. Trouble erupted between her and Baskin as soon as she became engrossed in the all-consuming task of filming Nuts, who was not participating in the production and felt himself an outsider in her life as she devoted herself day and night to the filming process.

Nuts premiered on November 20, 1987, to mainly positive but not overly enthusiastic reviews. She had produced one of the best performances of her career, one that should have elevated her to the same level as Meryl Streep's as an actress, but it never occurred, and Nuts did not fare well at the box office. Audiences appeared to be sending a message to Streisand that they did not want to see her in non-musical films, especially ones with such weighty subjects. She went to Aspen, Colorado for Christmas and New Year's with the Bergmans, depressed by the public's verdict on Nuts and with Jason in New York and intended to stay there for the holidays. And it was there that she reconnected with Miami Vice star Don Johnson, whom she had met briefly at that year's Grammy Awards and who wasted no time dragging her into a fast-paced courtship. It became a passionate affair in less than a week.

'I have to talk to people first if I want to meet them since so many are terrified by me,' she explained. 'So, if a person makes the first move [like Jon Peters and Johnson did], he's already one step ahead.'

He had grabbed her arm shortly after she arrived at a gathering, brought her to a secret nook, and then left early with her. He was seven years her junior, had lived his life quickly, and swore he had no regrets. 'I've done all I've ever wanted to do. The only things I haven't done are those I haven't considered.'

Johnson may be gruff, but as friends and coworkers attest, he "could have charmed Hitler." He was the blond, bronzed, manly gentleman with the physique of a beach lifeguard and a smile that could light up a funeral for any Jewish woman with Streisand's background. By the New Year, they were a couple, and by February, they were a couple.

'I'm thrilled, very happy,' Streisand told reporters. 'And I've never been very happy, so it's something I'm working on. It's as if I'm a kid again.' In the early days of her affair with Peters, she had expressed similar thoughts. In reality, the two men were comparable. Both were younger, brash, streetwise, had spent time in juvenile detention centres, and were aggressive in both business and sex. Johnson was also a talented athlete who excelled at golf, tennis, skiing, and powerboat racing. However, there was another side to his swaggering, macho, womanising persona. He was bright, sensitive, and, having suffered a huge sense of loss as a child as a result of his parents' divorce, he desired to settle into a tight family situation so that his kid, with his former lover, Patti D'Arbanville, would have a

54

true home with him. Although Streisand enthusiastically assisted in the decoration of his recently purchased million-dollar ranch house in Aspen and spent all of her free time with him, they did not share any of their own residences. Elliott, who was estranged from Jenny at the time, was living at Streisand's Malibu estate, a gesture Streisand made to assist him out, as she would always have a protective and close feeling for the guy who was her son's father.

When she was named the 'Female Star of the Decade' at the ShoWest Convention in Las Vegas on February 25, 1988, she arrived late to accept the honour, escorted by Johnson. Jon Peters was seated on the dais and rushed up from his seat to embrace each of them as they sat.

Never able to cut ties with the ex-men in her life, she let Peters arrange a party for her 46th birthday on April 24th, while Johnson was in Calgary filming Dead-Bang, an action picture. She flew to Ireland to be with him shortly after this celebration, lonely and seemingly head over heels in love again. She thought she had finally found a man with whom she might live happily ever after. They were taken with their arms linked and yearning to gaze on one another.

She and Johnson released a track called 'Till I Loved You' in mid-September. It ended up being their last song. Ten weeks later, Johnson and Melanie Griffith (one of his four ex-wives) revealed their intention to remarry, much to Streisand's surprise. Griffith had spent several months in an alcohol recovery centre after completing her renowned performance in Working Girl. Streisand was aware that Johnson had been meeting Griffith, but she firmly believed it was out of concern for Griffith's health and her battle with addiction, a scenario with which she sympathised. The entire world came tumbling down on her.

She had yet again failed to maintain a meaningful connection. She was the rejected woman this time, and she was furious with Johnson for terminating their affair in such a harsh, public way. For weeks, she urinated on him and the merciless press coverage that made her look like a fool.

The media's interest in Johnson's defection eventually faded, allowing her to devote all of her focus to a new project, a cinematic adaptation of Pat Conroy's The Prince of Tides. It would be another massive project because she would produce, direct, and star in the film. More than that, The Prince of Tides was about family and forgiveness, and she was at a point in her life where she thought she could forgive her mother for what she called 'emotional abuse' in her initial interviews for the project. It would reintroduce Jon Peters into her life as a guardian, the one who, after every studio turned her down on the proposal, would persuade Columbia to fund it for her. It would also result in a new, deeper bond between her and Jason, whom she would cast in the role of her son, as well as the realisation and acceptance of Jason's homosexuality.

As JASON'S PARENTS, Elliott and Streisand now had to confront something together. When Jason was twenty-three in 1989, neither he nor they had mentioned his homosexuality in public or, it appears, in private. Elliott has admitted to having a total block on the matter, and it wasn't until five years later, after Jason had gone public, that his father told English journalist Corinna Honan, 'Yes, [Jason] is gay. That's his choice, his business. It's something new to me, and it's a really delicate subject. But I'm not just sympathetic. I'm not sure if it's been a problem for Barbra. It's critical not to be prejudiced, because both of us are committed to him.'I simply want Jason to be happy and comfortable with himself, and to discover his own method of showing love. He could be a polar bear for all I care; he's as valuable to me as anyone. I told Jason a few years ago that I consider myself fortunate and grateful that we have each other. I told him how much I adored him. "I didn't always know that," he said. That I now understand."

Streisand and Elliott were privately and appropriately apprehensive while she was preparing The Prince of Tides for the cameras. AIDS was rapidly spreading, with cases doubling and then tripling each year. Was I to blame for his parents' guilt? 'I believe Jason's homosexuality is largely psychological,' Elliott responded. 'I suppose it's a result of conditioning... [I blame myself] for not being a more visible father. When we divorced, Barbra was awarded custody. I wasn't being fair to him. I left him alone in that surroundings. I believe he was affected by the lack of love at a critical juncture in his life, despite the affection and love grew subsequently. Barbra was preoccupied with her business and career, and I was just not present.

'I can't blame Barbra for attempting to be someone she isn't. I only have myself to blame. I know my intentions were good, but it's been a difficult road for Jason to overcome his lack of love. He's a really deserving and decent man. I believe he and Barbra now have a more mature relationship. She adores her son, and he is devoted to his mother.'

One thing that drew Streisand and Jason closer was his apparent sincere desire to become an actress, which had surfaced in recent years. She had seen him in several local amateur performances and thought he had a great talent. He had also appeared in three unreleased films that year. When Streisand first read The Prince of Tides, about the Wingos, a South Carolina family whose children grow up repressing nightmarish traumas, she thought to herself, 'Jesus, I'm perfect for this part [as the middle-aged Jewish psychiatrist, Dr Susan Lowenstein, who falls in love with her suicidal patient's brother, Tom Wingo]. I absolutely empathise with the woman, right down to the statement in the book that says she is in the process of ageing exceptionally well.' She also recognized herself in the traumatised Wingo children and in Dr. Lowenstein's connection with her moody, adolescent son, Bernard. Jason was living away from home in a small West Hollywood apartment at the time she began casting.

'Jason has never requested anything from me. 'He's never been ambitious,' she subsequently admitted. 'He has no ambition to be famous or anything like that, since, you know, being my kid and Elliott's son is tricky, with problems of competitiveness and all that. But then my son phones and says, "Mom, I hear you're getting ready to cast someone else for that role." I assumed you believed I'd be suitable."'

Streisand had cast a young actor, Chris O'Donnell (later to make a reputation for himself in Scent of a Woman alongside Al Pacino), who was a standout quarterback on his high school football team. 'Barbra showed me this boy she had cast in the part of her son,' she said. 'A very gorgeous blond boy,' recalls Pat Conroy, author of The

Prince of Tides. Of course, everyone in Hollywood looks great, but when I responded, "That ain't the kid," she said, "I already hired him." "That's still not him," I said. Bernard isn't a good athlete, and that's the point." So she browsed through the other youngsters she'd auditioned for. She eventually came to this one child. I had no idea it was her son. But he had a snarling, lovely adolescent aspect [and looked like Streisand, which had to have influenced the casting]. "That's the kid right there," I said. This happened, according to Streisand, when Conroy saw a picture of Jason on the piano in her living room. Memory is often elusive, taking up residence in places other than its initial circumstances. Whoever is accurate, the key issue is that Conroy saw Jason as Bernard before Streisand and when she was rejecting what seemed reasonable and right to others. Even after Jason was officially cast in the part, the news was concealed from the public and only revealed months later, when the film was already in production and on site. 'Deep down, I thought, "Well, it's dangerous." "We could both be attacked for this," she admitted.

Marilyn Bergman noted, "Every film she directs involves working out a part of her own life."

'I think she read The Prince of Tides seven times,' says Cis Corman, the film's executive producer. 'She was so familiar with the book that she would tell Pat what he had written on page 376. She could have become a rabbi after Yentl. Look, it's a difficult process for her, but it's not without delight.'

Working with Streisand on a film means feeding her fears. 'You have to keep telling yourself, "You're beautiful, you're wonderful,"' she says. Corman admits as much. Regardless, most of the performers who have worked with her will tell you how sympathetic she is to their difficulties, possibly because she is so aware of her own.

'A lot of this movie is incredibly relevant to me because it's about not blaming your parents,' Streisand stated at the time. We've all experienced a difficult childhood. However, blaming your parents keeps you the victim. The mother in me may make me a better filmmaker. 'Women may contribute a caring touch to a film,' Amy Irving said of Streisand as a director during the production of Yentl.

Diana, now eighty-two, was brought to the hospital with acute chest pains three weeks before travelling for South Carolina, where the film was to begin shooting, and only days before her forty-eighth birthday on April 24, 1990. Streisand was terrified. Work was put on hold as she stayed at Roslyn's side. 'It transformed my entire perception of the film's relevance,' Streisand admitted. 'The film lost its significance. 'My relationships with the people I care about become more important than the movie.'

Diana was now a senior citizen. She had been publicly chastised by her elder daughter and had never been able to refute or ameliorate Streisand's continual sharp pronouncements about the emotional trauma she had undergone at the hands of her mother. She had not been a showy or supportive parent, but she had done what she thought was right. She was unprepared to deal with the situation she found herself in following her husband's death, let alone nurture her daughter's "fancies." But Diana had never abandoned her daughter, no matter how caustic and cutting Streisand's accusations about her were to a press ready to capitalise on celebrity-revealing comments to sell their publications. Diana had inherited her own pain, an uncaring mother, and the dread that she would fail on her own. She was born at a time when women had far less opportunities for success unless they were beautiful, which she was not, and she had lost the husband she loved and been humiliated by the man she thought would provide a home for her children and herself. She was a victim of her time and her own shortcomings.

Streisand has fought her mother her entire life. There was an unbreakable cord beneath. She had always adored Diana. She had clung to her, slept in her bed for years after Manny's death, longed to make things right for her since her first achievement, needed Diana's acceptance and love more than anybody else in her life. She had a lot on her mind right now, and she was determined to let Diana know she loved her before it was too late.

With Diana on the mend, Streisand took Jason and roughly 100 cast and crew members to the small town of Beaufort, South Carolina. Pat Conroy had spent his adolescent years in Beaufort, where he would later teach English and coach football at his high school as his alter ego Tom Wingo. The town was named Colleton in the book, but Conroy had accurately portrayed it. Beaufort is located in the Lowcountry, where warm white beaches meet the south Atlantic. The village has a lovely natural harbour. There are dozens of inlets and rivers off the coast where small fishing boats troll for delectable gulf shrimp. To the north of town, high cliffs thickly forested with subtropical flora rise, and some of the surviving older buildings are composed of crushed oyster shells. Others, constructed high to keep cool, feature broad front porches and old-fashioned gardens with jessamine, oleanders, and wisteria mixed in with Spanish moss-bearded oak trees. The murmur of seagulls, the drone of heat-drawn bugs, and the nighttime cool had what Streisand described as a "quiet, mystical quality."

It needed time to build the necessary sets, thus the film did not begin shooting until June 18th. The first scene to be shot would be one of the final in the film, with Tom Wingo reuniting with his wife and three daughters after his romance with Dr Lowenstein in New York, walking with them on the beach, despite the fact that fifteen endings would be shot before that one was chosen.

Nick Nolte had been cast as Tom Wingo, deeply Southern, a man of great outer strength and inner turmoil, born into a dysfunctional family. His twin sister, Savannah, is a famous, gifted, troubled poet, and a suicidal patient of Dr Lowenstein. Caught up in her own difficult family situation– a philandering husband and a difficult teenage son – the middle-aged Lowenstein persuades Wingo to come to New York and help her to fill in the missing information that she hopes will unlock the mystery to Savannah's deep depression. During these voluntary, non-paying sessions, he reveals the hidden secrets of the Wingo family, which include an abusive father, murder and rape. Dr Lowenstein and Wingo fall in love and enter into a relationship which helps each of them to resolve their personal situations.

Both Warren Beatty and Robert Redford were previously discussed as possibly playing Tom Wingo, but neither was right for the character, who required a strong macho appearance, sensitivity and the ability to 'unleash torrents of raw emotion'. Nolte, at six feet one inch, 210 pounds, had a brawny, bruising physique. He was rugged, blond and raspy-voiced and his background had been rough and tumble. Raised in Omaha, Nebraska he had gone to Arizona State College on a football scholarship and transferred to three other schools due to poor grades and a low tolerance for alcohol. He turned to acting, supporting himself in the beginning as an ironworker. Fourteen years later he was still in touring companies, taking college courses whenever he had the time to obtain the credits he lacked for his diploma, and joining in the anti-war demonstrations that proliferated during the Nixon years. He was arrested and placed on five years' probation for counterfeiting draft cards with false information and married and divorced twice before, in 1976 at the age of forty-two, he made his first breakthrough as the co-star of the Irwin Shaw television mini-series, Rich Man Poor Man. He quickly became a popular Hollywood star known as 'a tough guy with soul and natural acting ability'.

Nolte had not fared well in his relationships with women and was at this time caught in a hostile divorce with his third wife. Streisand seriously had to consider if he might have difficulty taking direction from a woman. She decided to change the risk as Nolte projected just the right blend of grit and tenderness required for the role. 'In the movie, Wingo would have to come to trust a female therapist, while in real life he was going to have to trust me, a female director,' Streisand later said. This did not become the problem she anticipated. Nolte had a great respect for her.

'Barbra likes to explore,' he said. 'We shot some key scenes in several different ways. We also had long discussions about male-female relationships. It was the first time I had worked with a woman director. In working with male directors I've found that the male actor and director have a kind of collusive attitude about the emotional points of scenes. With Barbra, there is a lot of continued exploration.'

Their love scenes ignited sparks. 'I don't find it that easy to bare my soul, to do intimate things in front of a camera,' she admits. 'I'd rather do it in private. I had to yell, "Cut!" when things got too hot [with Nolte]. His make-up was all over my hair. You couldn't see my blonde streaks.' She had even more difficulty with appearing nude. She wears a scant nightdress in one scene after a great deal of discussion about it with Nolte and Cis Corman. 'I just find it rather sexier to wear sheer clothes in bed,' she defends. The love scenes she found most satisfying in the film were those that dealt with deep, mutual affection, Lowenstein cradled in Wingo's arms in a chair. 'The woman goes back to the safety of childhood again, being held by the father or someone who loves you,' she explained.

The act of touching someone's face, their hand, or being held, comforted by someone and being in their arms, had great meaning for her. In her direction of the scene where Wingo has his final catharsis she recreated her own visual memory of the time the touch of her therapist's hand on hers had caused her to open the flood gates of her emotions and weep. In a two-hour documentary laserdisc on the making of The Prince of Tides, which she narrates, she illustrated what she wanted Nolte to experience when Lowenstein takes Wingo in her arms, his head on her breast, as he wept after revealing the hidden secrets in his family. 'Oh, this is interesting, this is what it feels like to be held by your mother.'

The documentary is all about her directing approach to filmmaking, and while it is fascinating and insightful as to the reasons behind many of her choices, it also reveals the strikingly egotistical way she thinks of her work, the way she takes total control of its creative process. Throughout, the phrases 'I did this to the script,' 'I wrote that scene in my head over and again,' 'I rewrote,' and 'I improvised' are used. One may readily conclude that she wrote the screenplay entirely on her own. She never mentions working from a script adapted from his novel by Becky Johnston and Pat Conroy.

Despite their disputes on Yentl, she had brought Jack Rosenthal from London to Beaufort to "humanise the dialogue." He bit down on the thigh bone of a roasted duck one evening while they were working over supper in a Chinese restaurant, crushing his molar to fragments inside his gums. It was the least unpleasant aspect of the three weeks he spent "working with Barbra on the script," he claims.

She would spend hours on the smallest detail, driving her coworkers just as hard and as long as herself. Yet, difficult as she is in any work situation as a director Streisand is unquestionably sensitive to mood, to frame, to moment, and she has caught some extraordinary images in the film which she points out in the documentary - the Wingo house rising in morning mist from the marshes, the grace of the land, the view from Lowenstein's skyscraper terrace looking down on night-time New York City - but Stephen Goldblatt, the picture's cinematographer is never mentioned.

Then there's James Newton Howard's music. Streisand mentions 'Jim' in regard to music once, but does not elaborate on who she is referring to. She had a brief affair with Howard while he was scoring the film. They had been collaborating closely. Howard was a sensitive, handsome man, and there was a musical union of ideas, a time when they were 'breathing' together. It is a skill that both an accompanist and a singer can have. With the scoring completed, the matter concluded quickly, with no apparent resentments on either side. The atonal reverse of a theme to imply a character's alienation, the balletic piece that takes Wingo and Bernard through their football sessions - Howard provided a magnificent soundtrack that truly catches the mood of the film and often serves to describe the action.

Film is unquestionably a medium for directors. 'I appreciate seeing my visions come to reality,' adds Streisand. A director should not be one if he or she does not have a vision, yet without all of the magnificent technical, artistic, and creative talents that contribute to the final picture, a filmmaker would be paralyzed, unable to bring that vision to life, a world unto itself. Streisand's unwillingness to share or credit her coworkers stems from her total immersion in the film she is creating and her inability to think of it as anybody else's but her own.

She does, however, fully credit the famous violinist Pinchas Zuckerman, who can be heard dubbing the solos for Dr Lowenstein's virtuoso husband, Jeroen Krabbe (who beautifully managed the challenging fingering). Jason had one scenario in which he had to be seen playing Fritz Kreisler's challenging violin piece, 'Präludium und Allegro,' and doing so with great skill. ('I'd never touch a football if I could play the violin like that,' Wingo says.) He had three months to complete the fingering and movement exercises. He learned to play

'Twinkle, Twinkle, Little Star' after three lessons.'I couldn't stop giggling,' admitted Streisand. 'I know I wounded him, and I'm sorry, but he was so awful. 'However, by the time he had to play it in the scene, he was able to perform it like a young prodigy,' she added triumphantly. He had to soak his hands every evening since they were so stiff from practising. 'I knew my son could do it.'

It was difficult for her to direct her son. Jason was always well-prepared, always professional, and almost always cheerful. 'There isn't a bad bone in his body,' adds Streisand. He is, nevertheless, his mother's son and has strong ideas. They clashed several times. To his chagrin, Streisand had him replay one sequence over and over. 'You've told me what you want; now tell me what you don't!' he yelled. She tried, and eventually he recreated the moment exactly as she imagined it. The script called for him to walk off swiftly to catch his train in the final scene he had with Wingo, set in Grand Central Station, leaving behind the man who was a father figure to him and had helped him become a respectable athlete. After numerous takes, Streisand yelled at him, 'Walk like a man! Walk like a man!' implying that this was the point in the film when he would become an adult, but it seemed like a jab at the cast members.

While in Beaufort, mother and son developed a greater understanding and appreciation for one another. Jason performed admirably as Bernard, offering a genuine and empathetic performance. He is always accurate and credible. His eyes are dark, his hair brown and curly, and he looks a lot like his mother, but his large nose and full mouth distinguish him from Elliott. Slim at the time, of modest stature, with a captivating boyish smile, he never appears to be too old for the part.

During the filming, Jon Peters visited Beaufort. He'd recently remarried, and he and his stunning blond wife, interior decorator Christine, had adopted a young blonde child named Caleigh. Streisand agreed to be the child's godmother after being asked. Marriage and adopting a kid, ideally a girl, looked like a viable option to her, despite the fact that she had no significant men in her life. The Prince of Tides, on the other hand, had a large number of children in the cast, and she admitted that she enjoyed working with them more than any of the other performers. Tom Wingo had three young daughters, all of whom were played by talented children with whom she spent a lot of time. There were also flashbacks of Tom Wingo as a child, as well as his sister and brother. The three kid actors cast in the roles travelled to California with the group to shoot the brilliantly choreographed underwater swimming scene that gives the film such a magical image. Streisand devotes over half an hour of her documentary to these children's auditions and screen tests, as proud of their natural acting ability and attractiveness as she would be if they were her own.

'[I've been] considering how I want to spend the remainder of my life,' she explained at the time. 'I would like to work with youngsters. I'm missing children in my life. My son is now an adult. I've considered adopting a child, but I'm not sure I want to do so as a single parent. It wasn't too hot for me, and I don't want to subject another youngster to that.'

Viewing the film's rushes, it was evident that she was getting a fantastic performance out of Nolte and the other actors. Dr. Lowenstein is the one who falls short. Streisand's acting has a strained seriousness to it that frequently conflicts with believability. She is stiff, formal, and overly lighted in many two-shot or group sequences, almost pounding home the notion that she is in the shot. This is especially apparent in the scene where Nolte spots her across the room at an art exhibition and she looks to be standing in an aureole glow, making her presence impossible to overlook. 'I don't think about acting very much,' she defends. 'It's easier if you're playing by yourself. And I was extremely familiar with this persona.' The dual job of director and actress was a challenge she had handled brilliantly with Yentl, but much less so with The Prince of Tides.

'Barbra's talent for acting works against her abilities as an actress,' Nolte claims. 'Being a singer is a really lonely career that requires a completely different mentality. It's all about me as a performer. The lighting must be appropriate for me. [Entertainers] arrive on stage and don't know how to share. They are unwilling to stay for off-camera tasks. They have not been raised with a sense of teamwork. It makes it difficult for them to be taken seriously in the performing world. As a director, Barbra is far more tolerant. You don't have time to think about yourself, and she performs well in that situation.'

Streisand admits to having problems directing herself. 'When I direct, I become really tolerant and compromising, which is unusual for a perfectionist,' she explains. 'There is a kind of acceptance of things you can't alter that would be really beneficial in life. 'I live my life when I'm directing the way I want to live my life when I'm not.'

In late September, The Prince of Tides' photography was concluded. Now she worked long hours in the dubbing and editing rooms, like an artist on a canvas - 'Finishing a Hat, Putting Things Together,' as Sondheim had written. It would be fifteen months before it was released, her work completed, and the verdict rendered. She always stated she enjoyed the time between projects because it allowed her to potchkee around, shop, remodel her houses, read, read, read, and plan her next experience in filmmaking. She was refurbishing both her Carolwood Drive home and her New York apartment with furniture by Frank Lloyd Wright and Gustav Stickley. The walls were adorned with new paintings by Gustav Klimt and Egon Schiele. She was agitated.

She kept Caleigh overnight whenever she could in California. The tiny child, with her bright grin and golden hair, had completely captivated her heart. Caleigh was, in some ways, the winning child she wished she had and the daughter she wished she had. Caleigh was lovely, feminine, and open to receiving and giving love. She was very concerned for this outgoing youngster's happiness because Peters and Christine's marriage was already fraught with issues. Her impulse was to shield Caleigh from the fears that a divorced child would experience. She wanted to be there for her, recalling how she had not had such support herself. Caleigh made sure that her schedule was clean of other appointments on the days and nights when she was with her, which was usually once or twice a week. She would read to Caleigh in the evenings and stay with her until the youngster went to bed.

Her friendship with Caleigh was intriguing. After all, the youngster was her ex-lover's adopted daughter. However, Caleigh maintained a strong connection with Peters, who was a loving parent.

Furthermore, Jason's homosexuality made it unlikely that she would ever have a grandchild. 'I don't know,' one of her close friends replied, 'but I suppose Barbra feels she can relive her life via Caleigh - that is, the life she would have loved to have had. She's become a part of a fairy tale with Caleigh. Caleigh's world is all pink and lovely, or so Barbra tries to make it. You know she is always reliving the alleged sorrow of her upbringing. And yet, it is precisely this that has made her strong. Pain has that effect on people. Separates the wheat from the chaff. It distinguishes between those who have courage and those who are weak. Barbra had to succeed, and she did. And one thing is that she has never been ashamed of her past poverty and has always been proud of her heritage.'

Streisand has always had a strong affinity to her Jewish ancestors. Her work on Yentl strengthened them even more, as did her pride in Jewish history. Perhaps the only Hollywood star in history who has been openly proud of her Jewish heritage, she has never received enough credit for her choice to play Jewish women who could be admired - Fanny Brice, Katie Morosky, Yentl, all seminal roles, and soon in The Prince of Tides, Dr Susan Lowenstein. Culturally, whatever the public does not accept about Streisand, it accepts her Jewishness, and inherent in that acceptance is respect for her ethnic pride. It's a big part of what's made her the huge icon that she is. Her vulnerability is another feature that endears her to the people. She can make all the strong remarks she wants, but nobody believes her. A soft-hearted, empathetic woman lies beneath the occasionally stern exterior.

'She utilises her vulnerabilities and weaknesses as a seduction, like a laser beam,' Elliott says. It's really appealing, and it's part of her art. [However], her fragility is hidden behind glass, like one of those snowstorms in a globe that you shake. She has always mastered the art of playing weakness.' Elliott, on the other hand, emanates a pervasive impression of vulnerability and, since his breakdown shortly after their divorce, of someone who has lived a shattered life.

While waiting for the premiere of The Prince of Tides on December 11, 1991, she put together a four-disc autobiographical album Just for the Record..., a collection of previously recorded released and unreleased songs that allowed her to briefly tell her life story in the liner notes, giving her reasons for their inclusion and explanations about how they came to be made. The design divided her career into three decades: the sixties ('dedicated to the memory of Peter Daniels, who became my first accompanist'), the seventies ('to my beloved Gracie [Davison, her late dedicated housekeeper who had been with her since the time Jason was a youngster] whose laughter I still miss and to Howard Jeffries (sic), who would have liked this record)1 and the eighties ('to my mother who is 82 years old and still has a beautiful voice. And to Cis Corman, who has been my best friend from the 1960s, 1970s, and 1980s').

Putting this record together was a really emotional process. It starts with her first private recording of 'You'll Never Know' when she was thirteen and includes other previously unpublished recordings of songs she believed best conveyed the story of her career as a vocalist. During the production, she had Marty Erlichman call Barry Dennen to see if he would give her the tapes that they had argued over thirty years before. Dennen remained hesitant, but he could have caved if Erlichman hadn't returned to say that Streisand had changed her mind about joining them.

Several commentators have called Just for the Record... a narcissistic stroll down Streisand's memory lane. It is, indeed, a fantastic CD that provides the listener with a rare opportunity to hear the development, changes, maturing, and tastes of one of the world's best current song stylists. It also allowed Streisand to recount her story through lengthy written notes interspersed with over 150 photographs from her personal collection.

'She tosses a lot of stories around,' Hilary de Vries wrote of an interview with her just before The Prince of Tides premiere. '[Most of them] were written to present Streisand as a triumphant victim, one who makes art in the face of a deprived childhood, tyrannical directors, and an anti-woman industry. The effect, on the other hand, is of someone anthologizing her life as she lives it, examining herself from a short distance, with just the right lighting.'

'I'm simply looking for the truth,' she explained to de Vries, who was interviewing her for the Los Angeles Times. Of course, the question is who is telling the truth. Streisand's? Elliott's? Diana's? Jason's? Peters's? Who were the men and women she worked with during her long career, and with whom she shared her early years? She has regularly presented the same events to the media, fictionalising, embellishing, and recreating the memories in her mind in order to respond anew, analyse, relieve herself of guilt, or, in some circumstances, learn to accept it. The truth was frequently obfuscated, misrepresented, or dramatised, which is not uncommon for the creative, self-involved, or those who simply wish to charm, impress, or shock to obtain attention. When you repeat a narrative enough times, it tends to have its own truth, and Streisand was no exception. Her unhappiness as a youngster established a firm basis on which she and the public could understand where she came from and why she did some of the things she has done by repeatedly repeating stories about her deprived upbringing. It also gave her viewers their own interpretation of the woman they were watching, which provided another layer to her act, as it had done for two of her vocal foremothers, Billie Holiday and Judy Garland.

When she doesn't want to chat or answer inquiries, she likes to tell stories. 'I went to view the trailer for The Prince of Tides the other day. 'And when I'm in New York, I take a cab,' she said at the start of the de Vries interview. 'I don't have a 24-hour limousine service. I grew up in a poor home, and you don't think of hiring automobiles, but [I found myself suddenly very late]. And in a sweat suit - schlocky - which is how I dress most of the time, to be honest. Not exactly schlocky... So I started running because I couldn't find a cab. And it reminded me of my early days on Broadway, when I couldn't get a cab to my own play [Funny Girl], and I would beg folks on Central Park West - tears streaming down my face - to take me to Broadway...' There were always references to the past in such stories, never to the spectacular highs in her incredible life, but always to the sadness, the defenceless situations that were a part of her history.

The Prince of Tides received positive reviews upon its general release on Christmas Day, with almost all critics praising her talent as a filmmaker capable of eliciting outstanding performances from her cast. Her personal performance was repeatedly lambasted, which was a huge letdown for her. She had possibly taken on too much. If she had directed another woman in the character of Dr Lowenstein, The Prince of Tides would have been much better.

On her fiftieth birthday, April 24, 1992, she became impatient with herself. The renovation was over, and she had no particular man in her life. She was starting to feel her age, despite the fact that she looked a decade younger. And the men she was drawn to get younger as she got older. 'Poor baby, he's miserable,' Elliott observed. 'She keeps herself busy with so many things because she is frightened of failing. 'I'm terrified of the truth.'

'It's the mirror she has to face each morning, unadorned, make-up free, no attractive pink spots, no chance to cut and edit,' says one of her closest old friends. That is the source of Barbra's deep anguish. She can only be what she wants to be - that Hollywood glamour girl - through artificial methods. She is not a very good auty. I don't think she can or will ever be able to accept it. She notices crazy Barbara, the girl with the large beak, the hideous Jewish girl from Brooklyn, staring back at her. She does not and cannot see what we see - the unusual beauty hidden beneath her public mask. She's a unique species, a one-of-a-kind, and she has no way of judging. The fact that Barbra was not born gorgeous is both her greatest sorrow and her greatest privilege. That is something she may never be able to accept.'

auty. I don't think she can or will ever be able to accept it. She notices crazy Barbara, the girl with the large beak, the hideous Jewish girl from Brooklyn, staring back at her. She does not and cannot see what we see - the unusual beauty hidden beneath her public mask. She's a unique species, a one-of-a-kind, and she has no way of judging. The fact that Barbra was not born gorgeous is both her greatest sorrow and her greatest privilege. That is something she may never be able to accept.'

CHAPTER 7

There was discussion. Streisand had a crush on a young man, a 22-year-old tennis pro many years her junior and 28 years her senior. Even jaded Hollywood was shocked by the news. André Agassi, regarded as the "King of Grunge," made $11 million that same year. To the young people who came to see his showman style and killer skill, he looked and felt like a shaggy anti-hero on the courts, his dark ponytail falling below the back of a black cap, wearing scruffy clothes, black socks scrunched down over his tennis shoes, gold hoop dangling from his ears, and a Ché Guevara beard framing his striking face with its sharp features, bushy brows, and quick-shifting eyes. Adult tennis fans often greeted him with sneers, as if he were a bad Las Vegas lounge act. He'd broken the 'Mr Clean' all-white tennis uniform rule. He was a trendsetter and a valuable commodity in a sport that was losing adult involvement and audience. 'Agassi is tennis' marketing tool for the next generation of fans,' wrote Harvey Araton of the New York Times. 'He arrives MTV-ready, and if he turns a few parents' stomachs, his children will beg, "Can we get tickets for the Agassi match?"

'He's incredibly clever, very sensitive, and highly advanced - more than his linear years,' Streisand said in his (or presumably her) defence. And he's a wonderful person. He performs with the poise of a Zen master. It's very much in the here and now.'

Agassi was exactly where she desired to be today and tomorrow. She was fifty and middle-aged, but she perceived Agassi to be older than his true age and herself to be younger. This aided in closing the gap. He was vital, robust, moved like a gale, spoke like a hurricane, was cocky, confident, and unstoppable.

They met briefly during the Christmas holidays in Aspen, immediately following the release of The Prince of Tides, and began dating seriously in the spring of 1992. In response to a question regarding his friendship with Streisand, Agassi told the New York Times' Maureen Dowd, "I've been learning about the sweet mysteries of life, and this is one of them." 'I'm not sure I entirely understand. Perhaps she, too, cannot. However, it makes no difference. We came from quite different worlds, and when our paths intersected, we knew we had to spend time together right away.'

Streisand appeared upbeat and energetic. Her close friends backed her right to live her life as she saw fit. Jason was quite helpful. She was used to Diana's scorn and didn't care what Hollywood thought of her. The relationship was not as all-consuming as her more serious commitments in the past had been and while Agassi was off on the tennis circuit she occupied herself intensively in 'minding the store'.

The Prince of Tides was doing exceptionally well at the box office, having already paid for itself three times over, and was expected to be one of her most profitable pictures to date. Despite the fact that it was one of the five Best Picture nominees, she felt personally snubbed at the 64th Annual Academy Awards because her successful directing efforts were not recognized as one of the five nominated directors in that category.1 She bemoaned the fact that Hollywood would never welcome her simply because she was a woman.

Her denial by the business provoked heated controversy. 'Barbra was the first woman to actually wield authority,' said Lynda Obst, producer of The Fisher King, which received one Oscar nod (Best Supporting Actress, Mercedes Ruehl). 'Barbra caused way too much controversy at the beginning of her career. Her weight shifted. People are afraid to show their appreciation. They have a lot of business respect for her, but they also keep a certain form of affection away from her.'

Given that the film was nominated for Best Picture and seven other awards (including Nolte's and Kate Nelligan's performances as his mother but not Streisand's portrayal as Dr Lowenstein), it's surprising that she was completely overlooked. However, there are only five directors nominated, and as one Academy voter put it, "she was sixth good." Regardless, she took it personally and went public with her views. She emphasised that the final five directors picked were all men. They were also deserving nominees. The Prince of Tides, while beautifully photographed and wonderfully acted, was a flawed film. Streisand's directing touch is evident in all sequences in which she does not appear, yet because her role was significant, she was in a large portion of the film.

The Oscars and the controversy over Streisand's omission boosted The Prince of Tides' box office receipts. She remained enraged even when, only two months after the Academy Awards, Sony (which now owned Columbia Pictures) finalised a $60 million multimedia entertainment pact with her, one of the industry's richest deals to date. Michael Jackson and Madonna recently signed record deals with Time Warner for similar sums, but Streisand's included both albums and movies, as well as profit percentages, which significantly enhanced the basic price.2 Sony was also to keep distribution rights to her profitable thirty-seven-album catalogue, which had sold more than sixty million albums since 1964, the most for any recording artist during that time period.

'Barbra Streisand comes along once in a generation, so you hang on to her,' remarked Al Teller, former head of CBS Records (now Sony Records). 'Few musicians have a demonstrated track record that they can sing, act, write, direct, and produce,' says mega entertainment attorney Peter Dekom. 'Barbra is a threat in every area.' 'There are few entertainers who ever create an audience desire across both the music and film entertainment spectrum the way that Barbra does,' said Irving Azoff, then chairman of Time Warner's record company. She exemplifies style and refinement as well as commercial success.'

The industry thought she was being recognized and appreciated for her accomplishments. Streisand, on the other hand, did not see it that way. She would never forgive the Academy, and she recalled all too well how difficult it was to battle for tales she believed in, and how record executives made her feel as if she was auditioning the songs she wanted to put in her albums. Power meant complete autonomy, which she doubted she'd ever be able to demand. For years, she was the most powerful woman in Hollywood, yet the industry was still dominated by men. It was a barrier she couldn't overcome.

'Language provides us insight into how women are seen in a male-dominated culture,' she stated on June 12 on accepting the Dorothy Arzner Award, named for the trailblazing director/filmmaker. She went on to say, 'A guy is dominating, a woman is demanding.'A guy is forceful; a woman is pushy. 'A man is unyielding; a woman is a ball-breaker.'A male is a perfectionist, while a woman is a pain in the ass. 'He is assertive, while she is aggressive.'He plans, and she manipulates.'He is the leader, while she is the one in charge.'He's dedicated, she's obsessed...'A multi-talented hyphenate is someone who acts, produces, and directs. She's been dubbed conceited and narcissistic.

'It is believed that a man's reach should outstrip his grasp. 'How come a woman can't do the same?'

She concluded by telling the assembly of film professionals, "We are a remarkable breed." We are the hood girls - sisterhood, that is... Nature intended for us to be creators, to give birth... Let's make photos that depict life not only as it is, but also as it could be. Let us channel our collective feminine energy into creating films that represent our maternal inclinations and releasing them into the world. Because the world desperately requires it.'

She was never a company- or studio-owned artist, and her autonomous behaviour, as well as her seeming feminist advocacy, made her a constant target for criticism by the Hollywood 'boys' club. The establishment accused her of being a perfectionist in a business that requires compromise. Such charges irritated her. 'Perfection is... a kid when it is born,' she reportedly retorted. 'Perfect is an understatement; it's a miracle. It's the Almighty. It's incredible. It's more than ideal. Nonetheless, it shits and pisses. Everything appears to break apart sooner or later, therefore there is no such thing as perfection.' What she desired was to be permitted to follow her own convictions, to do the finest work she was capable of doing, to produce a film in which she was proud. It had to be done her way in order to be successful. Hollywood has a business mentality. It was hesitant to invest in anything that had not yet proven to be a box office success. If it could, it would have turned her into an ethnic Doris Day, starring in the same formulaic musical until she was forced to retire due to time constraints. Streisand had refused to be packaged, frozen, and marketed like an ice cream bar by a studio, and she would not let the films she chose to direct, produce, or both be consumed by the system.

She was as headstrong and indomitable now as she had been as a child, choosing controversial subjects for future films that would only complicate her ability to secure full studio funding to supplement the development monies provided by Sony. To a Violent Grave: An Oral Biography of Jackson Pollock by Jeff Potter, released in 1985, she obtained the rights with Robert De Niro's Tribeca Films, about the difficult relationship between the iconic abstract artist and his wife/manager, Lee Krasner. De Niro's late father was a painter, and the project featured him and Streisand in two supporting roles. She acquired the rights to a tale about Lieutenant-Colonel Margarethe Cammermeyer, who was forced to resign from the Washington National Guard after admitting to being a lesbian. She was offered a screenplay, The Mirror Has Two Faces, written by Richard LaGravenese, who had also written the scenario for The Fisher King, and became involved right away.

The Mirror Has Two Faces, a Tri-Star project, was partially based on a 1959 French film starring Michelle Morgan about a plain, unattractive lady who starts again after plastic surgery. LaGravenese's version of the story was more nuanced. In his script, a plain woman with poor self-esteem is transformed as she discovers her own inner beauty, the message becoming: self-love physically affects people's appearance. The storyline and characters still required a lot of work, but it was a project that allowed her to reflect on some of her personal experiences.

Her desire to create The Normal Heart remained unwavering. She regarded the Kramer play (and Colonel Cammermeyer's narrative) as being about people's right to love whomever they want - about tolerance, acceptance of other people's lifestyles, and not being punished for being who and what they are.

There were rumblings among the activist LGBT community that she, as one of Hollywood's top stars, had not done enough for AIDS. Elizabeth Taylor had already stood forth as the liberal Hollywood AIDS spokesman. They wanted to know where Streisand was. They argued that she had only provided $350,000 to AIDS research and treatment in 1991, with the majority of that going to children suffering from the disease. However, this is an unwarranted and unkind critique. Streisand endowed academic seats in women's studies at UCLA, cardiovascular research at UCLA, and another at the Environmental Defense Fund. Her Streisand Foundation continues to give more than $1 million to civil liberties, environmental causes, and AIDS research each year. And she was frequently motivated to add huge sums for other causes and disasters, such as the Valdez oil spill, as they occurred. She believed that as an advocate for the LGBT community, she could accomplish more if she could develop a commercial film that would reach a big audience and represent them as being like everyone else in their need for and right to love. She had personal motivations as well. Of course, Jason's homosexuality was a factor, but Stan Kamen, a close friend and her agent at William Morris since she and Sue Mengers had split up, had recently died from AIDS, and she had been deeply saddened by his death, as well as the frustration of knowing there was no medical cure for the plague and that research resources were limited.

This was several years before the film Philadelphia, starring Tom Hanks in an Academy Award-winning performance, broke the Hollywood taboo on AIDS-related stories. Philadelphia, on the other hand, concentrated on an AIDS patient's right to continue working rather than the character's right to love. Hollywood was not yet ready to delve into this subject. With The Normal Heart, Streisand would continue to confront headwinds. Renegotiations for the rights with Kramer began in the spring of 1990. This time, everything went much more easily. Both caved a little, and a compromise was achieved. Kramer would draft the script, but she would have the last say. He flew to California yet again for story discussions at her home. Both had evolved. 'She was a softer person, also more cognizant of how hard she had been on herself in the past,' Kramer reflected. 'She talked a lot about it, about not always striving to be the perfectionist. She had been in the type of therapy where you connect with your inner child. She was more thoughtful, softer in certain ways.'I had known I was HIV positive for two years and assumed I would die soon. My doctor in New York called me in an emergency the first week I started working with her. I'll never know how he acquired Barbra's phone number. But my blood test had just arrived, and he called to tell me that he needed to start me on AZT right quickly and asked for the name of a drugstore in Los Angeles where I could start right away. I was distraught, and Barbra was wonderful, consoling, and organised all at the same time. I'll never forget it, nor will I forget her. She wrapped her arms around me, called the pharmacist, and we talked.

'I was vehemently opposed to AZT. There were different schools of thought regarding whether it was safe or not, and I was hesitant to take it until we got more medical information. So this was a significant emotional event. Also, AZT can have terrifying adverse effects on your body, and I thought to myself, "Holy shit!" I was terrified that I would have these skin sores and be unable to function well, and this was what I had hoped for for years - for Barbra to return to the project.'

Kramer says that when his doctor called from New York, Streisand knew it was bad. 'She said if you want to converse discreetly, go to the bathroom next to her study. I was shaken as I walked out, and she asked, "What's the matter?" And I informed her. Then she wrapped her arms around me and embraced me close to her. I was deeply moved. 'I couldn't keep my tears from falling.'"How are you feeling?" was the question from then on. How are things going? "Are you experiencing any side effects?" There was a lot of warmth. It's a far cry from 1985, when I felt more like a hired hand. Fortunately, the drug helped, and I had no adverse effects, so I continued working.Barbra writes in the traditional manner, describing every shot and angle. She wants to know what the camera is doing, what you start focusing on, where it moves, and what the action is so she can follow it. She is the type of person that questions everything. Why has a comma been removed if you had one there yesterday and don't have one today? And she knows, because she remembers a comma there. She has a low filing cabinet, really an open drawer, with every scene from every version of the script that I, she, or anybody else has written. It is divided into scenes, and she will remember which one had which and will continuously compare them. Then she will record the exact sequence she desires on tape so that there is no room for error. I'd then clean it up and deliver it to her the next day.

'We'd labour from three-thirty in the afternoon until eight or nine o'clock at night. The rest of the house had been redecorated. There were new paintings and a lot of mission furniture, but the study stayed mostly the same. She was always stunning. She has incredible skin, her eyes are a clear blue, and her hair always looks good, even when it's simply hanging. She wore the same clothing to work every day - fancy jogging suits.

'There's something extremely lovely about her. She is quite vulnerable. You can sense it, and whether she opens it up to you or not, you are in its presence. Perhaps it is what great vocalists have. They can sing these songs about how the world or love has touched them, and you want to tell them, "It's all right." And she recalls everything the press has ever said about her. I asked her why she clung to things for so long, why she couldn't let go, and she said, "I can't seem to help it." How do you go about it? You've received a lot of criticism. "How come it doesn't bite the shit out of you?"

'"Well, it used to," I explained, "but you can't have a strong opinion about something and not expect to offend someone, somewhere." "Let it go, let it go," I kept saying. She is attempting to be everything. To be the most ideal and admirable person possible. People remark about her desire for power and control. Control is a harsh phrase to describe how people use it against her. She has the right to run her business her way. As an example, consider the following. "There are things you write that I can't put on the screen," she said. "Give me an example," I inquired.

' "Well, the scene where the two men make love believing they have engaged in safe sex and there is a spot of semen on one of the guy's chest, and they don't know whose it is and one of them indicates that it could be poisonous."

'"That's what I wanted to demonstrate. That a slip like that may be fatal. It's quite moving, in my opinion." "You can't show semen on someone's chest," she said simply and definitively.

Her affair with Agassi ended abruptly. She had gone to Wimbledon in June to witness him play Pete Sampras in the quarterfinals and had excitedly cheered him on. Agassi was defeated in the match. By September, he was dating a younger woman and would soon marry the actress Brook Shields, who was his own age. There was no other male in Streisand's life at this period. Jason was in New York, attending film school at New York University, where he had made a short film in which his father and grandmother, Diana, appeared, which had received critical acclaim. He was now focusing on a career as a writer and director rather than acting. Streisand stayed in Manhattan for a while. She was lonely,'very lonely,' according to close pals. Jason was afraid of heights, a relatively new phobia, and couldn't ride the elevator up to the rooftop apartment. This meant they met in more impersonal settings, such as restaurants or other people's houses.

'I think, weirdly, Barbra wants to make The Normal Heart for Jason,' Kramer explained. 'I believe it is her way of battling for his acceptance and the right to love who he wants and be proud of who and what he is. It's the ultimate present, the best of the best. If she's nervous about something, that's where the anxiety comes from. It's difficult to make a film on homosexuality when your son is involved. Also, I believe that when the film is completed, it will include more information about Jason because he wants to work on it. He has exceptional taste, and I believe Barbra and Cis Corman admire him.'

Jon Peters and his wife Christine were getting divorced. Caleigh, who was only three years old at the time, was Streisand's concern. She associated strongly with the child and shared her confusion at being the victim of a broken home. Her bond with Peters remained strong. He and Christine both saw Streisand's participation with Caleigh as a stabilising force in her life. Streisand designed a bedroom for her in the Carolwood Drive mansion, a story-book room in pink and white with pristine organdy curtains and shelves brimming with books and dolls. The toddler was clearly attached to Streisand and delighted in her company. Peters was in charge of her care, but Christine also had custody. Caleigh was still too little to comprehend how Streisand's engagement in her care and rearing would affect her. Caleigh and Streisand, who are naturally affectionate, embraced and kissed frequently. Caleigh referred to her as 'Baba,' and Streisand lavished attention on her. 'I want just the best for her, the most love and devotion that I can give her,' she told close friends, who noticed Caleigh's delight. 'She considers Caleigh to be her own. 'It's incredible how much she adores that youngster,' one observes.

In a society where children have so little influence over their lives, she had always been a champion of their issues. Caleigh brought this subject to the forefront of her mind.

'I started singing her a lullaby one night as I was putting [Caleigh] to sleep,' she recalled.On the treetop, rock your infant to sleep. The cradle will rock as the wind blows. The cradle will tumble if the bough breaks..." "Will the cradle fall?" she exclaimed. What was I supposed to say? 'I mean, that's a terrifying concept to tell a youngster.'

She developed a garden area with a sandbox and slide, as well as a playhouse where Caleigh could enjoy lemonade and cookies with a friend in the afternoon. Caleigh had playmates because she invited children from her preschool to the house, she took her to the beach where they built sand castles together, she went shopping with her for clothes, allowing the child's taste to guide her purchases, and she accompanied her to the paediatrician for her regular check-up, holding her hand so she wouldn't be scared. Many things may be interpreted from her deep attachment to the charming blonde toddler with blue eyes and a broad smile. She was the child she wished she had been, the girl she had always desired, the cord that would bind her to Peters, the grandchild she might never have. The most obvious explanation, however, was that Caleigh met Streisand's need for ongoing connection with another person.

Streisand returned to politics in the summer of 1992, after Bill Clinton secured the Democratic nomination. Michael Dukakis had not energised her in the previous election. She now worked tirelessly for his victory alongside the Bergmans, as impressed with Hillary Rodham Clinton as she was with her husband. Finally, there was a very astute possible First Lady, reminiscent of Eleanor Roosevelt, one of her long standing inspirations. Mrs Clinton appeared to understand the home issues at stake - AIDS research, health care, a woman's right to choose abortion, the plight of the environment - and would not be afraid to speak out to bring them to the attention of the people.

She met the Clintons on the 16th of September at a HWPC fundraiser hosted on the enormous lawns of reclusive film mogul Ted Fields'

$39 million, 49-acre Beverly Hills house, one of the top five national Democratic donors. It was her first public performance in six years, and it was on a show crowded with Democratic supporters from Hollywood, including Warren Beatty, Annette Bening, Goldie Hawn, Whoopi Goldberg, Stephen Spielberg, Candice Bergen (wearing glasses), Jack Nicholson (in shades), Michelle Pfeiffer, Dustin Hoffman, Richard Dreyfuss, Danny DeVito, Rhea Perlman, Dionne Warwick, and Mike Nichols and Elaine Clinton was presented by Beatty, who appeared to be overcome by the great crowd and their passionate expression of support.

'Warren Beatty said he hadn't known me for a long time, but I was sitting there thinking I had known many of you for a long time,' he remarked during his speech. I've seen your films or sung your songs and thought that life could be as it appears in the words or on the screen.' 'I have always longed to be in the cultural elite that others reject,' he added.

Streisand, dressed simply in a black scoop-necked, long-sleeved Donna Karan gown with her hair carelessly combed loose to frame her face, received a standing ovation as she approached the microphone. 'I was prompted by the Chernobyl accident six years ago,' she told the Hollywoodites who had raised over $1 million that evening. Now I'm spurred by the prospect of another disaster: George Bush and Dan Quayle re-election.' She sang 'On A Clear Day You Can See Forever,' followed by 'Happy Days Are Here Again,' before a roaring throng.

Perhaps they were. As a committed Democrat, it appeared like for the first time in sixteen years, someone with whom she could identify had a decent chance of winning the presidency. She had a strong attraction to the man. He had the kind of charisma she adored, and he listened to his wife, women, and ordinary people. He was the type of man she might easily grow attracted to. Later that evening, they talked for a bit. He explained to her that his father died before he was born, and that he realised she had lost her father at a young age. 'It has the ability to alter your entire life,' he said.

'Yes,' she said. 'It's a difficult thing to overcome, and I'm not sure you ever do. It stings to think that mine never found out I was renowned or accomplished anything worthwhile. But the fact that you are on your way to becoming President is difficult not to disclose.'

Clinton smiled down at her and nodded, and they were joined by several others eager to shake the hand of the man they hoped would soon be President of the United States.

CHAPTER 8

'How come no one has criticised the Republican White House for its association with Arnold Schwarzenegger, Charlton Heston, and Bruce Willis?' Streisand reacted angrily to a reporter's question about whether the alleged Hollywood-Clinton connection posed a threat to "the very fabric of this Republic." Her man had won, and she was there for the pre-inauguration and post-inauguration festivities, as well as having a front-row seat as he took the oath of office. The final banquet of Clinton's inaugural week, hosted by 19,000 guests at the cavernous Capital Center, drew a large Hollywood contingent. The massive celebration was derisively dubbed a 'Hollywood-Washington production' in the press. Streisand performed 'Evergreen' while the President and First Lady held hands. Then, with a thunderous applause from the audience, she gave her all to 'On a Clear Day You Can See Forever' and 'Happy Days Are Here Again,' the latter receiving five standing ovations that did not stop until she introduced the President-elect, at which point the entire crowd stood up, all at once, whistling, hurrahing, and clapping.

Streisand passed the microphone to Clinton, who was standing on stage in front of a white lighting with a black seat from her act behind him. 'Thank you for sharing my last night as a private citizen with me,' he said before turning to Streisand, who was still standing on the stage, and giving her a warm, tight bear embrace.

One staff member who had previously worked on the Reagan and Bush pre-inaugural galas described the Democrats as "much more fun, much more casual." There are no prima donnas in the room. There will be no ozone layer spraying over everything. Four years ago, every gown appeared to be red, white, or blue. This year, the brighter and funkier the sequins, the better.' In contrast to the sparkling evening gowns worn by Goldie Hawn and others, Streisand donned a dramatic three-piece pin-striped Donna Karan suit, the floor-length skirt slashed to the thigh dubbed 'the peek-a-boo power suit' by the Washington Post.

Karan, America's leading female designer and now one of Streisand's closest friends, had designed a fresh, daring, sophisticated style for her. Not only did the two women share a love of fashion, but they also shared many of the same political and social beliefs. They belonged to 'the sisterhood,' a group of women who, like Streisand, competed in a male-dominated environment. Karan was gorgeous, middle-aged, and headed a stunningly high-profile design firm. He was tall, dark-haired, and nicely built - trim but not model-thin. However, the financial backing for her venture came from businessmen who were more concerned with the bottom line than the designer's need to express herself creatively, a predicament that Streisand also faced when directing movies.

The Washington Post attacked Streisand once more, this time for what it dubbed "Clinton's wooing of entertainment royalty," adding that movie stars were "incapable of serious involvement with the politics industry of Washington." Streisand was picked out as a prime target and derogatorily referred to as "La Streisand."

'It felt as if I was being told how dare I seek to penetrate a man's territory when I directed a movie,' she told a Los Angeles Times journalist. It's now: "How dare I be interested in politics?" Please excuse my tone; I am outraged!'1

Streisand enjoyed the thrill and excitement of the momentous occasion despite the unprecedented meanness of the press. She stayed at the Stouffer Mayflower Hotel, which was quickly dubbed 'the power hotel of the week' by the press, as other guests included President Clinton's mother, Virginia Kelley, her husband Dick, Clinton's brother Roger, Mrs Clinton's two brothers, Tony and Hugh Rodham, Vice-President Al Gore and his family, political guru James Carville, Barbara Walters, and a long list of top film, concert, and television performers. Streisand was also dubbed "the woman quickly becoming the top celebrity."

The next day, 20 January, she sat teary-eyed at Bill Clinton's inaugural ceremony, the weather fresh and cool, a winter sun lighting the podium as he was sworn into office, his broad, usually smiling face sad on this occasion. The new President seemed to be surrounded by a youthful aura; after all, he was only forty-seven, a year older than John F. Kennedy when he was slain. This was the core straightforward reality that Streisand had come to see in

Washington. A man she trusted was about to take the oath of office as President of the United States. It was a pivotal moment that marked the beginning of a new era. She had high aspirations for the country's future. She who complained so much, who felt so much Jewish guilt, developed a negative attitude, saw the black side rather than the white, the half-empty glass rather than the half-full, who claimed to be scared and afraid so much of the time, felt positive. She could directly relate with the Clinton administration. She felt like an insider, as if she belonged.

This would usher in a new era in her life, one in which she would speak up and become an activist. 'We [Hollywood executives and actresses] have the right to be considered as seriously as automobile executives,' she told an interviewer when one of the media referred to her as "the princess of tides." 'No one would dispute the president of G[eneral] M[otors] talking to individuals in Washington,' says the president.

'a cheerful thumbs up and wink from out-going President Bush through a limousine window as the car pulled away from the White House; Mrs Clinton and Mrs Bush chatting amicably as they raced through Capitol corridors towards the West Front; Clinton stooping to pet Millie [the Bushes' dog] when the Clintons arrived at the White House; Chelsea, unable to suppress a yawn even during the v She was captivated by these personal reminiscences and in awe of the history she saw at every step. In just a few days, she had been a part of that history. The concept excited her, instilling in her a powerful sense of patriotism comparable to her pride in her gender and origin.

And she was escorted to the various events by a handsome escort, ABC TV anchorman Peter Jennings, a distinguished-looking news reporter with a self-assured demeanour and huge popular appeal who had recently divorced his wife. Streisand may have seen in him some of the same qualities that drew her to Pierre Trudeau: knowledge, political and global understanding, combined with good beauty and tremendous charisma. Eleven official inauguration balls were held. Streisand, dressed in a grey jersey Karan gown ('trimmed down to here and slashed to there,' attended the most high-profile event, the

Arkansas Ball at the Washington Convention Center, with Jennings, leaving just after the Clintons.

According to the Washington Post, Streisand presided over the after-the-ball Inauguration Day party at the posh Georgetown Club. Jennings had to return to work, and she arrived with Donna Karan. The only people who were not present were the President and First Lady. Jack Nicholson's wicked laugh could be heard. Warren Beatty and Annette Bening cha-cha-ed, Lauren Bacall cha-cha-ed, Jack Lemmon, Kathleen Turner, Chevy Chase, Shirley MacLaine, Robert De Niro, and Richard Dreyfuss were present, as were a slew of Kennedys and well-known politicians. Streisand, 'wearing a long black hooded cape that made her look like Marie Antoinette escaping revolutionary Paris,' fled through the kitchen, the bar, and out the front door at 1.30 a.m., with Karan hard at her heels.

Streisand's connection with Jennings would remain 'simply close friends,' despite the fact that she relied on him for inside information on many of the things that she was interested in. They communicated frequently and met whenever she was on the East Coast. Her obvious and persistent public criticism on topics prompted the media to announce that she was preparing to run for political office. She made it quite obvious that she had no intention of running for office; she was simply an engaged citizen. Much attention was paid to the rumour that she had the President's ear, which she categorically refuted. She was invited to the White House Washington Correspondents' Dinner in mid-May 1993 and then "granted 5 minutes with Clinton." 'I told him about what was being done for AIDS research,' she said. 'A few of us from the entertainment business were invited to the health-care meeting a month ago. We didn't even meet Clinton for dinner. We later ran into him. We had dinner with his mother, whom I admire since she is such a strong, positive woman.

'There was all this criticism that Hollywood people were entering into areas where they were not experts, but we were called to the White House for communication ideas - we were brought there for them to tap into our communication talents - how to get a message across to the American people. We've been referred to as "airheads" and "nitwits." This is completely unjust. And it's tarnishing our community's principal industry. It is indicating that there is no brain present. Was the entertainment industry responsible for the national debt?'The media is currently in a Hollywood-bashing frenzy. They mocked the fact that Janet Reno and I have dinner to "hash out issues." It's beyond me why two renowned, hard working women, separated by their positions, would not wish to talk to each other. Why the hostile reaction to folks from Hollywood? Why do we pose such a threat to the media? We have the right, as an industry, as individuals, and as professionals, to be treated as seriously as executives in the automobile sector, an industry that is struggling to sell its products abroad. On the other hand, we produce something that the entire world wants to buy, which helps our balance of payments, creates jobs, and pays a lot of taxes.'

On this occasion, she strolled the Capitol like a visitor, visiting the Smithsonian and Monticello. 'The most moving moments were being at the National Archives, holding the Emancipation Proclamation and the Louisiana Purchase, and seeing the film at the Holocaust Museum about the survivors who were reaffirming the preciousness of life, struggling to maintain their dignity, and helping one another to gather strength to survive,' she admitted. They did not succumb to cynicism, which is hurting our country and prevents us from coming together.'

Nothing could stop her from speaking her mind. She was and had always been pro-choice, for women's equality, for environmental protection, a devoted liberal. 'That's why I have a basis to back up my convictions,' she told Los Angeles Times reporter Robert Scheer. 'That's how I pay it forward. That is how I express myself. And, whether right-wing conservatives like it or not, I will continue to raise it.'

Sammy, a fluffy white bichon frise with black button eyes and a friendly personality, arrived in early January 1994. She hadn't owned a dog in many years. Sadie, whom she admired and thought she would never be able to replace, died before she completed A Star Is Born. Sammy was right on her tail wherever she went in the house.

The cataclysmic earthquake she had always feared would strike Los Angeles appeared to have arrived on the morning of January 17th. She awoke in the house on Carolwood Drive to the sounds of breaking glass and wood creaking, as well as the house groaning and trembling. The first thing she did was rush out of bed, cautiously avoiding the glass from a nearby smashed window, and desperately scream out to the tiny puppy. 'He was so quiet he soothed me,' she added when she discovered him sitting under her dressing table. She then called her mother's number, who was terrified but unharmed. Fortunately, no one in the house was hurt, but it was a scary experience, and she had lost many of her prized items of pottery and glass.

She had recently completed work on a new album, Back to Broadway, which contained many of the songs she had been unable to record for the original Broadway album. 'Everybody Says Don't' (Anyone Can Whistle), 'Children Will Listen' (from Into the Woods, and perhaps Sondheim's most important song), 'Move On' (Sunday in the Park with George), 'I Have a Love', and 'One Hand, One Heart' (West Side Story, lyrics only - a duet with Johnny Mathis) were all performed. However, Sondheim's influence on the recording sessions was not as strong this time. She performed two brilliantly executed songs from Andrew Lloyd Webber's yet-to-be-released Sunset Boulevard, 'As If We Never Said Goodbye' and 'With One Look'.

Sunset Boulevard was in rehearsals for its West Coast premiere, and the English writers who shared credit for the lyrics, Don Black and Christopher Hampton, were in town. She requested that some minor adjustments be made to the lyrics of 'With One Look' and 'As If We Never Said Goodbye' to better suit her needs (as Sondheim had done with 'Putting It Together' on the previous album), and she asked Black and Hampton to meet her at the Carolwood Drive mansion to discuss it.

'It was the pinnacle of my professional career,' says the author. Black, who also worked with Lloyd Webber on Song and Dance and Aspects of Love, as well as writing the lyrics to 'Born Free' and many other hit songs, was emphatic. 'She is a fantastic storyteller with a tremendous instinct for lyric phrasing and expression. It was every songwriter's desire to have a song performed by Barbra Streisand.Christopher, myself, and Andrew's musical director, David Caddick, who was also on Sunset, travelled together. Christopher couldn't stay long because he had another commitment, but he was eager to meet her. We went to her residence as a group of three. As we approached the gates, it appeared to be a small residence. It wasn't the long driveway you imagined as the entrance to a home belonging to a celebrity of her calibre. Inside, it was a different story; wonderful flavour, but not what you'd anticipate. What exactly would that be? Shangri-La, I believe.'She was running late. She had gone to the dentist since an issue with a tooth had suddenly arisen. It was mid-morning on a very sunny autumn day. Her secretary greeted us and made us feel at ease in the living room, which included a piano in one corner. We waited around 30 minutes. Christopher was about to leave when she walked in with a sisterly demeanour. "Hi, hello everybody," she said, greeting everyone as if they were relatives. I was shocked by how common she appeared. She was dressed casually, wore almost no make-up, and wore tennis shoes. "How are you guys for tea, coffee?" she inquired. There was no sense of being in the presence of such a famous woman. It was incredible. Christopher left after about five or ten minutes of chit-chat, leaving just me and David Caddick at the piano. He didn't say anything for hours on end because he wasn't asked to.

'She sat across from me and started offering goodies like potato latkes, olives, and nuts. On the table between us, she'd move a dish closer to me. Meanwhile, she forensically studied the lyrics. "With One Look" was her main preoccupation.

'"Will people understand what I'm saying?" she wondered. "It's about a silent movie star, as written." People will hear it on the radio or on tape, and if they haven't seen the program, they won't understand what I'm saying.``She wanted to include some clarification in the verse. That did not sit well with me. "Songs from musicals are specific," I explained. We talked about it for quite some time. There was nothing contentious, bossy, or demanding about it. She was accommodating, but we went over each comma and crochet in the song. Finally, I said, "Well, let me think of something." Her secretary then interrupted with some paperwork she needed to sign, sandwiches were brought in, and I used the time to write some lyrics for the song's opening. I believe they said something along the lines of "They don't want me anymore, they all say I'm through, but it's time they knew - With one look" and so on. My objective was to establish right away that this was a celebrity who had passed her peak but was still stubborn.

"There's a poem that says, "One tear from my eye makes the whole world cry," and she wanted "one tear in my eye makes the whole world cry." I admired her zealous commitment. She was obsessed with every detail. The session had a relaxed collaborative vibe about it. Very friendly. This went on for hours, with David remaining poised at the piano, extremely respectable. Eventually, she said, "Well, maybe we should try it."She was now seated next to me on the couch, sipping tea, when she set the cup down and sang the first lines of "With One Look" without standing or turning off the piano. This incredible voice emerged. David discovered her key and backed her up after the first few bars, and it was incredible. This ordinary-looking woman was drinking tea and singing liquid diamonds in my ear. I'd had enough goosebumps.

'"Well, what do you think?" she inquired. "Is it all right?" For years, I haven't sung. I haven't done a concert in a long time. "Do you really believe it's okay?"

She was so insecure, so unsure of herself, and it was just amazing. There was no acting. I held the highest regard for her. When we finished the session, she played some of the songs she'd already recorded for the CD and told me how Sondheim revised everything for her. I understood why he did it. She gives lyrics new life and interpretation. She is without a doubt the best singer of our time. "Does it sound like it's mixed right here?" she'd ask as she played the recordings. "Did you hear the breath?" - more like a new singer starting out. There was no question in my opinion as to why she had remained at the top. Because she does not release a record; rather, she reveals it.

'Andrew had agreed that I should work with Barbra, but I was still nervous, so I showed him what I'd done. You're up against two icons. How many people are in each stratum? It would have been disastrous if Andrew despised it but Barbra adored it. It would be a nightmare that no one wants to think about. But Andrew thought the lyrics were appropriate for her situation. Finally, he produced the tracks and worked on the recording arrangements.'

Black was also present when she recorded the two Sunset Boulevard tunes. He was overjoyed with the first take, and even more so with the second. She went on to do another twenty or so."Oh my goodness!" I said. Don't keep singing since this voice won't stay!" The engineer then plays back the identical line from each of her takes. She has a sheet and marks which phrases or words she likes best from each. Then she has them assembled. It's a miraculous sewing work, a surgical skill. "I like the breath on take number twenty-two," she said. And you're sitting there, it's just mind-boggling.'She desired various musical phrases and would sing them to the trombonist or trumpeter, saying, "You know it would be very nice if you could play something like -" and then la-la a few notes that took on an instrument sound. She is one-of-a-kind.'

Back to Broadway soared to the top of the charts almost immediately after its release, inspiring Streisand and Marty Erlichman to believe that the moment had come for her to return to the concert stage. Her previous appearances in front of a live audience had always caused her "great misery... every night I was terrified." 'Then, on April 24, 1993, Donna Karan gave me a fantastic birthday party, and Liza Minnelli got up to perform, and I was sitting there thinking, "How does she do this?"' she says. "How does anyone sing in front of a crowd?" I could never force myself to sing in front of people at parties. Because there is a black curtain out there, I can sing on stage. I can only see a few people, which bothers me. So simply seeing her captivated me, and it became a challenge. I didn't like having to face that fear. I am afraid of many things, but what I hope is good about me is that I am afraid.

'"Why can't I do this?" I wondered. Besides, so many of my admirers wanted me to perform live. People told me, "You owe it to them." It was beginning to bother me.'

'I had returned to London,' Don Black recalls, 'and Alan Bergman called me and said Barbra wanted to open with "As If We Never Said

Goodbye" and would I make some changes [not made for the record], to make it more relevant to a singer who was returning to the concert stage after a long absence. "I'm not sure why I'm scared. I'm familiar with the area. Norma Desmond, with the cardboard trees and the painted sea..." I altered it to "the band, the lights, familiar sights..." and other minor changes, then faxed it to Alan, who faxed back Barbra's ideas. There were also six or seven phone calls. Again, the smallest of details.'

The song had personal significance for Streisand, who had begun her career in live venues - cabaret and the stage - and had grown more afraid of continuing to appear in these settings. That concern had not vanished, but a concert tour would significantly boost her recording possibilities. The inevitable spin-offs would be a record album and a pay-per-view TV special (eventually discarded in favour of a Home Box Office special), which would generate enormous income.

She was preoccupied with money. She was wealthy, but not wealthy enough to accomplish anything she desired without regard for her future. There were the non-commercial films she intended to make, as well as her foundation and the other profoundly felt issues for which her financial support, even if little, could make a difference. On a more personal note, she was redecorating her New York apartment with precious American eighteenth-century antiques and paintings, this time in response to a private visit to the White House that she remembered well.

She told Tom Shales of the Washington Post in December 1991 that she was considering a tour for financial reasons. 'I'm actually out of money because I don't work very much,' she admitted. 'I've purchased all of this land [California beachfront property], and I can't sell my other land [the Malibu ranch], so I may have to go out and sing just to pay for my house.' The ranch was proving to be a huge strain on her finances. The taxes were costly, and the upkeep, with the extensive grounds and five residences on them, was massive. The land has also served its role in her life. Each house had been decorated as if it were a movie set. She was eager to move on to the next assignment once she had completed this one. Her interest in art deco and art nouveau had waned. She desired funds to purchase primitive and Early American paintings, as well as arts and crafts furnishings. Negotiations with Christie's auction house for a public sale of some of the ranch's goods began.

Kirk Kerkorian, the owner of the new $1 billion, 5,000-room MGM Grand in Las Vegas, called Erlichman in August 1993 and, thinking he might entice her with the offer, proposed to donate $3 million to her favourite charities if she would make a one-time appearance - New Year's Eve - at his hotel less than two weeks after the opening of the world's largest hotel-casino project. The offer arrived at a good moment. Her film efforts were on hold for the time being since, as she puts it, "the show was to be on New Year's Eve." I despise New Year's Eve. It's a lonely night for me... it's never a good moment. There is so much pressure to be happy. So I thought, 'What a terrific way to spend New Year's Eve... putting on a performance.'

Kerkorian's offer provided Streisand with the ideal chance to begin a live concert performance. She, on the other hand, had no intention of appearing without private compensation. Erlichman pitched Kerkorian a contract in which Streisand would sing at the MGM Grand for two nights, December 31 and January 1, earning close to $10 million for each performance;2 also, the shows would be filmed (with the best rendition of each song being used) for television. Kerkorian quickly agreed to the higher terms, knowing that Streisand's attendance could be the entertainment coup of the decade. Other name artists, such as Paul McCartney or Michael Jackson, might bring a throng, but their attendance would be less remarkable because they had toured extensively in previous years and had been seen on cable television.

Everything else in Streisand's life was placed on hold while she began working with the Bergmans on her appearance concept. Her plan was to use music and film snippets as milestones to take the audience on an autobiographical journey through her life and career. She would not only write the majority of the script, but she would also direct it, and she wanted to be surrounded by people she could trust - Erlichman, Cis Corman, the Bergmans, and Dwight Henion, who had produced so many of her television specials.

She asked Marvin Hamlisch, who had collaborated with her on The Way We Were twenty-one years before, to be the conductor. Hamlisch had received a third Academy Award for his adaptation of Scott Joplin's music for The Sting, as well as four Grammys, a Tony, three Golden Globes, and had composed the music for the Pulitzer Prize-winning show A Chorus Line, as well as They're Playing Our Song and The Goodbye Girl.

'I didn't need the job, but I would never have turned it down,' he says. It seemed like the correct thing to do to me. I also thought her return to the stage after twenty-seven years would be a historic event, and I wanted to be a part of it. I just assumed I was born to do this. When I was asked to consider the scenario - conducting for Barbra - I considered it a privilege. We're talking about a fantastic voice... and a fantastic lady.'

Early October saw the release of tickets for two New Year's Eve shows at the MGM Grand. According to Erlichman, the telephone provider did not want the Las Vegas tickets to be available during the week because they were concerned that incoming calls would overload the system. Over a million requests were received on the first Sunday, with only the first callers able to purchase seats. Streisand was taken aback by the outpouring of support. Although she was terrified of the enormity of such an enterprise, of suffering tremendous stage fright, of forgetting her lines and lyrics, an idea grew in her head that Las Vegas could be the starting point for an international tour.

For years, she'd been used to scripted speech shot in short bursts and knowing that if she said something wrong, it could be reshot or altered later. Finally, she agreed that if she was well-prepared and could use a tele-prompter system large enough for her to view from the stage, it would be beneficial, but the musicians, technicians, and venues have to be the greatest. Erlichman went on a lengthy trip to see the arenas and concert halls in some of the major cities he thought would be the most viable for her, and she began rehearsals on Columbia Pictures' largest soundstage, the same one where she had recorded the songs for Funny Girl and Funny Lady.

Her first goal was to have the sound for her live performances as precisely controlled as it was in the recording studio. She hired one of the country's finest acoustical experts, Bruce Jackson, who had worked with Elvis Presley for six years and Bruce Springsteen for ten. 'I had heard she was difficult to work with,' Jackson explained. 'She definitely kept everyone guessing. If you disagreed, you had to remain firm. She'd listen and try to shake you. You were dead if you showed signs of being rattled and gave up ground. She was demanding, but I discovered that if you give her what she wants, she is a terrific delight and highly stimulating.'

'She understood what she wanted, but she didn't know how to get there,' said Tom Gallagher of Aura Systems, which was producing a custom speaker system for the concerts. 'It was our responsibility to keep testing until we got it right,' says the author.

Streisand desired an intimate, controlled sound, which would be difficult to accomplish given the scale of the arenas where she would be performing. After numerous fruitless suggestions, Jackson ultimately suggested that carpet be spread on the floor and thick drapes be hung on the walls of the music halls. 'I thought it would be prohibitively expensive, but when I proposed it to Barbra and Marty, they both replied, "Yes, do it."'

A 64-piece orchestra was to accompany her. Donna Karan was designing the two outfits she would wear in the two sections of the concert so that she would not only look stunning but also move freely. When she wasn't needed, she listened to meditation cassettes to keep herself as calm as possible. The entire effort was as focused and meticulously orchestrated as a Broadway production. The Columbia rehearsals were her out-of-town try-outs. There was nothing left to chance. Every line she was going to say on stage had been practised to near perfection.

'Barbra would tell me these anecdotes [about her past],' Hamlisch recalls, 'and I'd say, "Put it in the show." She has a beautiful way of putting the facts out there, almost with whimsy, and you realise she is one of us. She is this person with this incredible gift, but she speaks to us as if she genuinely cares. The show was crucial in allowing her supporters to see her for who she is.'

The days leading up to the first event, which took place on New Year's Eve, 1993, were chaotic. The Grand Garden arena of the MGM Grand Hotel held over 13,000 people. For security purposes, all but one of the doors leading into the arena were sealed, which meant that 13,000 people had to line up single-file, airport-style, and pass through metal detectors (designated VIPs were whisked through a back door). Tickets ranged in price from $50 to $1,000, with 4,000 seats at the top level costing more than $500 per person on average, and some fans having paid brokers three and four times face value for prime seats. Would they be enraged now that they had to wait in line for up to an hour to take their seats? And would this result in a grumpy audience that would be tough to woo in the first few songs of her set? Streisand examined all of the options and decided that she couldn't appear unless she felt safe, so she would take the chance.

On New Year's Eve, the masses were filled with excitement as they waited to pass through the security checkpoint and enter the arena. The show was supposed to start at 8 p.m. Around half-past, eight white stretch limos converged on the curb. Cheers erupted from the audience as each celebrity walked out. Liza Minnelli, the President's mother (an avid gambler and Las Vegas fan), Coretta Scott King, the widow of slain civil rights leader Martin Luther King Jr, Prince, Quincy Jones, Michael Crawford, Alec Baldwin, Kim Basinger, and Streisand's former directors Peter Bogdanovich and Sydney Pollack were among those in attendance. No one seemed upset that the celebrities did not have to wait in line. 'I never thought I'd see her live in my life,' said one woman who had paid $500 for her ticket and had been waiting since 6pm. Another person concurred. 'I had no choice but to be here. What if she doesn't feel at ease on stage and decides never to perform again?'

As soon as she stepped onto the stage at the MGM Grand, she could hear the tremendous roar of the audience and realise that while directing movies was her love, the stage was the only way she could achieve immediate fulfilment. And she was about to face the harsh realities of her life. There was no one in show business who could compete with her, not Frank Sinatra, Michael Jackson, or Madonna. She was no longer merely a celebrity. She was a living legend.

CHAPTER 9

She stood outside her dressing room, away from the backstage chaos that had erupted in the final few minutes before her show. Her deep-cut neckline on her black gown perfectly framed her petite, voluptuous form. A dazzling display of jewels hung around her neck. Her shoulder-length light brown hair, streaked with blonde, was combed loosely and softly. She directed the three members of her staff who were hovering around, still caring for her hair, make-up, and gown, to step aside with a tiny wave of her left hand. The regal gesture was instantly obeyed. For a little period, she stood still, alone, her famed chalky white undulating hands clutched tightly before her, the only visible sign of her uneasiness - graceful fingers like those of a Shiva goddess, lengthened nails flushed with lacquer.

The stage manager, a tall, broad-shouldered young man in a business suit with a dark-haired ponytail, approached her. He kept a walkie-talkie close to his mouth. 'Give the house lights a flash,' he murmured into it, signalling the arrival of the star. People would be hurrying to their seats right now. A minute later, the house lights were commanded to be turned down.

He gave Streisand two minutes.

She took a step forward. She took a brief draw as the young man at her elbow offered her a lighted cigarette and walked her cautiously over the cable-strewn area to the bottom of the backstage staircase that she would have to mount to reach the strange balcony set. Several members of the staff were gathered at the bottom of the steps, one of them held out a paper cup full of cold tea as she approached. She leaned very close and drank it with a straw. The overture was coming to a close. The 64-piece orchestra, conducted by Marvin Hamlisch, was located to her right, where she and the audience could see it, though a curtain hid the space where she stood. Hamlisch turned to face her, and she nodded, indicating that she was ready. The music grew louder.

This was the moment she had been dreading. She inhaled deeply, closed her eyes, and lifted her chin as if straining for air.

'To one side, please,' Streisand's pony-tailed escort instructed the workers as he assisted her up the somewhat steep flight of steps leading to the higher level of the set. 'We're on our way to the stage,' he announced over the walkie-talkie.

The audience in the front row was ecstatic. The air was filled with applause. The orchestra was playing the first few lines of Barbra Streisand's classic "Happy Days Are Here Again." She halted for a bit before continuing up as the attendant straightened the skirt of her long gown behind her so she didn't trip as she got to the top.

'Are you ready?' he questioned as she approached the door.

'OK,' she said behind her back. 'Happy Days Are Here Again' ended on a high note. The curtain was drawn back, and Streisand strode out to a tremendous ovation, her head back and a big smile on her dazzling face hiding her underlying anxiety.

She stood on the balcony area to the stage left of the massive proscenium, the orchestra visible behind her through the palatial, columned, two-story living-room set's tall, faux windows. One end was bordered by a fireplace, the other by a balcony. The stage was furnished with French-style chairs, tables, and sofas, as well as stunning arrangements of white flowers. She appeared to be pinned in the radiance of the aureole spotlight. Someone in the audience cried, 'Come on, Barbra!' and she stepped closer to the balcony rail, still smiling. The Grand Garden arena was enormous in size. People continued to applaud and cry out to her. As she gazed out at the sea of blurred features, she remained steady and gracefully calm. As the faint beginning bars of 'As If I Never Said Goodbye' were heard, Hamlisch raised his baton, and the crowd fell silent. All eyes were on her as she stood in the light, her anxiousness visible, a hesitation in her demeanour. The entire audience seemed to lean forward, as if to communicate to her that they were reaching out to her.

'I'm not sure why I'm afraid,' she sang in clean, pure tones, Don Black's altered lyrics appearing to represent her own thoughts.

Her voice rose to an exciting conclusion. There was startled quiet, followed by frantic applause, shouting cheers, and a standing ovation. She stared out at the sea of faces and the tangle of arms reaching out to her. Her anxiety had started to fade. The crowd's shout swept over her. Her peers' careers had come and gone, and they had come and gone again. She had maintained her popularity on her own. She couldn't help but know that this was true in the midst of such adoration. Her lips curled into a smile.

'Aren't you sweet? 'What a beautiful audience,' she murmured in a slow, deliberate voice that was so well-milked that her words were audible even from the farthest corners of the enormous arena where the cheering persisted. Her Donna Karan gown was split to the knee on one side, exposing a shapely leg as she moved across the platform. She lowered her gaze to the front row, where she introduced the President's mother, Virginia Clinton Kelley, and Coretta Scott King. Then she continued with her performance, which was essentially a one-woman Broadway production based on her childhood fantasies, connections, family ties, and social standing.

The off-stage voices of numerous imaginary analysts, male and female, were used in the concert format, allowing her to travel back in time to her upbringing in Brooklyn, her love affair with cinema - and with Marlon Brando. His image was shown on a huge screen in a scene from Guys and Dolls, looking young, vital, and attractive. Streisand, at the age of eleven, replaced his starring woman, the lovely Jean Simmons, in the tape and sang with him the fascinating Frank Loesser song 'I'll Know'.

Jason, Elliott, and Caleigh sat near the stage on Jon Peters' lap. An entire page of photographs of herself with the little girl was featured in the program, and she spoke directly to her from the stage about the bedtime stories they read together before dedicating "Someday My Prince Will Come," Caleigh's favourite song, to her, with pictures of the two of them projected on the giant screen behind her. This was followed by a touching rendition of Sondheim's song of loving protection, 'Not While I'm Around,' sung to Jason and backed by images from their past. At the end, she kissed him and whispered, 'I love you.'

'I love you, too,' he said. Her eyes misted as she bowed her head. Never before had she so openly expressed her feelings for her son, and both Jason, who was sitting next to Elliott, and the audience were moved. There was a unique impression that the performer and the audience had touched each other, had private time together, from this point forward. Their cheers and silence were personal expressions of their affection for her. Between songs, she sipped tea, fidgeted with her hair, brushed it away from her face. But every word she said and every song she sang were projected on giant closed-circuit television screens deliberately placed and visible from practically every angle to the audience as well as to herself. At one point, she realised she had jumbled up the lyrics of 'Evergreen,' and a shocked expression clutched her face. She'd misheard the cue. She froze for a split second when Hamlisch and the orchestra marched behind her. Then she laughed sheepishly, 'And it's my own tune!' She went on, the orchestra playing in unison under Hamlisch's direction.

She returned after intermission in another Donna Karan ensemble, this time a white tuxedo jacket worn over a floor-length skirt split hip high on one side. It was modelled after the pin-striped gown she wore to the pre-inauguration banquet, which prompted one female critic to remark sarcastically that "even a strong, successful woman has to play the femme fatale role."

Mike Myers, a comedian from the popular satirical television show Saturday Night Live, came running up on stage cross-dressed as his 'wickedly funny alter ego', a Long Island housewife with a Streisand obsession, and shouted in a deep, affected, feminine New York-eese accent, 'Barbra, don't listen to that woman!' Streisand laughed naturally and teased Myers as he described her complexion as 'buttah' and her nose as' something to die for'.

The optimistic philosophies in the final three songs, 'Happy Days Are Here Again,' sung while historic clips were shown on the screen, 'On a Clear Day You Can See Forever,' with its affirmation of a positive and bright future, and the poignant Bernstein-Sondheim classic, 'There's a Place for Us,' were highly successful in the closing segment. Streisand had made the show feel tailor-made, as if the words had been created only for her. Of course, this was true for 'As If We Never Said Goodbye' and Sondheim's 'I'm Still Here' ('occasionally a kick in the rear, but I'm here...'). One day you're praised for blazing tracks, the next you're chastised for your fingernails... Who does she think she is, a man producing? 'maintained my toes and my space, I kept my nose to spite my face...').

Some of the songs' interpretations could be criticised. She didn't seem to be able to convey the underlying meaning of the 'doormat' or 'victim' songs. 'Can't Help Lovin' Dat Man' stopped short of absolute sacrifice, while 'Lover Man' failed to capture a young girl's yearning. Even 'The Man Who Got Away,' which was wonderfully performed and overshadowed Garland's legendary mis-accents, appeared to elude her grasp. 'My Man' was a bigger hit for her. When she eventually departed the stage after many bows, the audience erupted. The large amphitheatre, which had been filled with the vibrancy of her voice and the power of her personality before she left, was silent, despite the sounds of the milling masses as they left.

They referred to her as "divine," claiming that there was "not one wrong note" in her performance; in fact, she had hit a flat top note in "The Man Who Got Away." Being present at the first concert in Las Vegas was historic in and of itself. People from all over the world had flown in. 'You come all the way from Sydney just for this concert?' inquired one woman. 'Yes,' she said. 'She hasn't sung in public in - how many years? - twenty-four or twenty-seven? What if this is the last time she appears? She is the best singer to have been born in my lifetime. There is no one who can compete with her, and there never has been.'

She had rarely communicated with her audience with such immediacy. 'When Streisand sings, her mastery of the audience lies in her regal calm; she distils her own feelings,' wrote Pauline Kael in the New Yorker. You get the impression that she doesn't need the audience and that she could sing with the same compelling intensity if she closed her eyes. The voice of Barbra Streisand is her own instrument.' This was correct. However, she had exposed herself to an audience while maintaining her distance, a skill that great politicians such as Roosevelt and Churchill possessed but is lacking in many artists.

After the show, she pounced on Erlichman, Hamlisch, Henion, the Bergmans, and Cis Corman with questions about the sound system, teleprompter, images, and lighting - all the technical aspects she felt were faulty. 'Was the neckline of my dress too revealing?' she asked a close friend who came backstage. My mother will have a seizure.'

She was glowing the next night. Celebrities in the audience included Michael Jackson, Steven Spielberg, Gregory Peck, Mel Gibson, and television personality Jay Leno. The audience response was much more fervent than the previous evening. 'Tonight was exactly how I had dreamed it would be,' she remarked later at a reception in her huge hotel suite. 'Everything felt right,' she says.

Her attitude reflected the high she had gotten from the concerts. The monetary benefits were fantastic. The two events made more than $12 million, exceeding her predictions and more than doubling the earnings of any prior pop or rock concerts, which attracted up to 90,000 attendees. Of course, no celebrity has ever charged such high amounts for tickets. Then there was the performance memorabilia, which ranged from $100 bottles of Streisand-signed champagne to $25 T-shirts and had already produced more than $1.5 million.

She told Erlichman she was ready to go out on the road after dealing with her stage fear and finding a feasible means to protect herself financially so that she could go with the initiatives near to her, both commercial and charity, without too much anxiety for the future. He was to finalise planning for the projected tour, which would begin in April 1994 at the Wembley Arena in London, travel to Washington DC, Detroit, two stops in California - Anaheim and San Jose - and conclude at Madison Square Garden in New York City. She'd be on the road for several months, and there would be many anxieties, pressures, and demands to deal with outside of, and because of, the tour - the films she wanted to make, her recording contracts, and her private concerns for her mother, who was nearly crippled from arthritis, Jason, Caleigh, and 'the age thing'. She was in her fifties and had become a showbiz cliché: the big performer without a man in her life, unable to take her cheering audiences home with her at night.

She wanted to move on and simplify her life. 'I appreciate the concept of evolution and change,' she said. Between ever-increasing costs and devastating bush and forest fires in the Malibu region, she had decided to abdicate responsibility for the ranch, and negotiations were initiated for her to donate it in its entirety to the Santa Monica Mountains Conservancy for a conservation institute before leaving for Las Vegas. This would improve her tax situation while also relieving her of the burden that the ranch presently represented. She then decided to sell the majority of the belongings of the five ranch houses. She had time before going to England to choose what she wanted to sell at Christie's in Manhattan. The decisions were frequently challenging. She felt emotionally attached to many of the pieces. 'When it was difficult to relate to humans, I could relate to inanimate items,' she said of her extensive collection. 'They didn't argue with me, and they didn't think I was insane. As a result, we had a fantastic friendship. I also enjoy being surrounded by lovely things. But I'm in a better place now. I can relate to others, have relationships, and own things. They are now less valuable to me. It has to do with psychological development and a shift in priorities.

'I'm feeling like letting go. I don't want anything in storage. I don't want them to be in boxes in the basement. If I don't have a place for them anymore, I want others to enjoy them. It's nice to utilise these things for a while and then pass them on during your lifetime,' she continued.

However, Streisand's insatiable urge to construct situations for herself was indicative of her entire nature. Everything had to be just right. She had a perfect vision of everything.

'I would never place a black vase in a grey-and-burgundy room,' she explained. She preferred monochromatic decor and avoided wearing designs. She preferred 'black and white movies, and the family photographs on the piano in the living room are black and white - colour photos would upset the harmony.' Even the candy wrappers in her candy dishes had to be colour-coordinated.

Christie's scheduled a two-day auction on March 3 and 4, with 535 lots, some of which had several objects. Each piece was appraised, and the lowest acceptable bid was agreed upon. Streisand had meticulously recorded the prices of each item. If the listing was removed or unsold, Christie's would still charge her a fee, which had to be considered. On the other hand, it was a celebrity auction for the corporation, a publicity coup worth a fortune, and they traded this off to Streisand's favour when calculating the cost of the sale. Because of the nature of their provenance, celebrity sales always brought greater prices for particular goods.

She received widely distributed, free publicity through an extraordinary deal with Architectural Digest, which did not normally carry a photo piece on houses or furniture for sale. On this occasion, they consented to reveal a portion of the ranch collection that was to be auctioned, and at Streisand's request, the exquisite Tamara De Lempicka painting, Adam et Eve, was emphasised with her on the cover. The magazine photographers came on the property immediately after her return from Las Vegas and worked on the shoot from early in the morning until late at night for over a week. Christie's packers came not long after they were dispatched. Streisand kept a careful eye on both surgeries.

Included in the sale with the De Lempicka (estimated sale price $800,000–$1 million), were her cherished 'Peony' ($300,000–$400,000) and 'Cobweb' ($800,000–1 million) leaded glass Tiffany lamps that she had bought and paid for on the lay-away plan when she was first appearing on Broadway, the two antique cars ($50,000–$65,000), an exquisite diamond and jade Cartier clock ($100,000–$150,000), an amazing assortment of art nouveau glass and furniture, art deco bronzes, silver and furniture, along with a host of memorabilia and less important items.

During the auction, which attracted international attention, she remained in Los Angeles. She was taken aback when she learned the value of her collection - about $6 million. The more valuable items sold for close to what they were appraised for, but the items in the second day of the sale - the memorabilia whose value depended on how much the public was willing to pay for something that belonged to Streisand - sold for ten to fifteen times what was expected.

She left for London and the first leg of her tour with this fantastic news. The English press splashed giant headlines about 'The Selling of Barbra Streisand' before she even arrived. Never before had there been as much pre-performance publicity focused on the astronomical ticket sales for the four shows she was to do (the 12,000-seat arena was already sold out for all performances) and the fact that many had changed hands at ten times their face value a week before the first concert.1 Selfridges, the Oxford Street department store, set up a Barbra Streisand Boutique with everything from a £10 coffee mug to a £300 wool-and-leather embroidered jacket; in between, there were watches, mugs, posters, scarves, purses, totes, T-shirts, polo shirts, and baseball caps - almost all with her picture and the concert logo, which she helped design with Sony Music, her merchandising agent. In addition to these apparent moneymakers, retailers carried reissues of the majority of her albums. Wembley Arena would also feature multiple stores selling the same products, and the concert program, written with her assistance, would cost £13 ($20), with a 45 percent royalty paid to her.

Marty Erlichman, Cis Corman (Marvin Hamlisch had arrived earlier to rehearse the orchestra), and several members of her staff - secretary, hair stylist, make-up artist, dresser, and a bodyguard - accompanied her to London on Concorde, arriving late Sunday evening, 17 April 1994, a historic date for her because she had never performed in concert in Great Britain before. She emerged sleepy-eyed behind her tinted glasses, dressed comfortably but not elegantly in a brown-leather jacket, baggy pants, wedgee scuffs, and a wool beret, and was met by an entourage of police, senior airport officials, airline VIP representatives, and concert promoters, as well as over fifty members of the press and a host of fans. She munched an apple as they made their way through the crowds to a waiting Daimler limousine that would take them to the Dorchester Hotel, where she had a £1,000 a day suite filled with the white and yellow flowers she adored (especially tulips) and pre-stocked with the Queen's and her own favourite bottled water, Malvern, boxes of Reese's Peanut Butter Cup chocolates, and Hershey mint bars.

'I don't like being famous,' she told her interviewer the next morning on early morning television. I dislike having the reporters following me around. I dislike talking about myself, and I want to be remembered for the work I do, not for stories about me or what others think of me. It's just not something I enjoy - the deafening acclaim of the audience. It has no effect on me. I want to please people and give them what they want, but I feel like I'm achieving that now with my movies and records.' Her welcome in Las Vegas, on the other hand, had had a profound effect on her, leaving her on a high for several days thereafter.

Nothing, not even earlier visits to London, had prepared her for the British press. It wasn't so much the large number of them following her every move - she was used to it - as their dismissive, disdainful attitude. She was front-page news in almost all the many daily papers except the Financial Times, and the articles featured every possible negative - she was pampered, difficult, money-hungry, 'the most steely woman on earth', dressed 'decidedly down-market', and had the Wembley Arena fully carpeted because she thought it would be 'too draughty' (no member of the press having thought to ask the real reason for the last 'idiosyncrasy'). She handled it as lightheartedly as she could.

'You have to get this properly,' she gently reminded one journalist. 'The British call it Strei-sunned. My name is pronounced with a gentle "s" like the sand on the beach. Stry-sand.' On Tuesday afternoon, in between rehearsals at Wembley, she appeared in the car park for a charity event, handing over the keys to one of fifty Variety Club Sunshine coaches (her personal donation) to transport disabled children to holidays and events they would otherwise be unable to attend. A pretty dark-eyed child gave her flowers. 'Flowers, oh, flowers,' she murmured, her eyes welling up with tears. She would, in reality, donate $10.2 million from the proceeds of her tour to charity.2

She was too busy rehearsing, making sure there were no hiccups in the first concert, which was just twenty-four hours away on Wednesday night, April 20. When she had a spare moment, she would meditate alone. She was afraid that the British reviewers would be harsh on her, that there would be a general group reaction to her American bravado, feminist beliefs, and wealth. They'd come to hear her, their 'attitude' with them. She couldn't and didn't want to change. She was who and what she was, and that was the end of it. You can take it or leave it. But she could do it all - sing, perform, and look her finest. She practised until the orchestra was too tired to continue. Her constant busyness distracted her from thinking about the moment she would take the stage for the first time. Stage fright struck her once more. She listened to meditation recordings, attempting to maintain a cheerful attitude because, as she put it, "I easily get sidetracked into this abyss of fear and I have to get myself out of it." The harsh pre-concert press had severely irritated her.

What she may not have realised was that the more she was attacked by the media - both American and British - the stronger her grasp on the populace became. 'She is a role model - the living proof that if you believe in yourself, you can do anything,' insisted a fan who had purchased tickets for all four Wembley shows. She had a difficult upbringing, but she was determined to succeed. She is an inspiration to all of us.' 'Her mother told her she was unattractive and couldn't sing,' said another. The press is often critical of her, but she is a natural survivor.'

Her frequent accounts of her miserable background, her perception of being unattractive, her unstable love affairs, and the media attacks made her appear vulnerable and lessened the distance between her and her fans. 'She is living proof that you can do anything,' remarked one of her admirers. 'She would have been a secretary if she had listened to her mother,' The Times' Giles Coren agreed. 'That early rejection is very important to English supporters, and [Wembley] will be a display of solidarity as well as entertainment. They'll show up in droves to show Barbra's mother how wrong she was.'

Streisand took a few minutes before the show to contact Diana. Diana told reporters, "She said she hoped I'd be able to see the show when it comes to Los Angeles." 'I said I hoped so as well.' These were not the words that her daughter desired to hear. Her desire to achieve, her voracious ambition, her want to be renowned, to be recognized as someone had always gone hand in hand with her desire for her mother's approval, a display of maternal arrogance. She would never feel successful until she had it. The irony was that Diana's apathy had spurred her to become a megastar, which was why she was never pleased with her achievements and always afraid that one misstep would destroy everything she had earned.

CHAPTER 10

Before she ever sang a single note, she received a five-minute standing ovation. She wiped tears from her cheeks with the back of her palm, a rare public display of emotion. The audience was finally seated again, and she sang her opening number. The presentation was nearly identical to the Las Vegas concerts, with the exception of some chit-chat about England and the English that was not spontaneous - every phrase was projected in front of the audience on the autocue.

'This is a very special night, very special to me,' she murmured, and the words rolled across the prompt displays. 'People question why I'm on the road for the first time in 27 years,' she continued. 'Hey, if you came from California with the earthquakes, mudslides, and fires, you'd be on the road as well.' She took a drink of her favourite herbal tea. 'I love England, especially cucumber sandwiches with the crusts off,' she remarked, eliciting a few titters. Some video footage of Princess Margaret at the opening of Funny Girl twenty-eight years before was played, as well as further clips of Prince Charles welcoming her backstage, all of them looking remarkably youthful. 'Who knows, I might have been the first actual Jewish princess... Princess Babs,' she quipped. 'I can imagine what the newspaper headlines would have been like. "Blintzes Princess Plays the Palace" as well as "Barbra Digs Nails into Prince of Wales!" ' The sound of genuine laughter could be heard this time.

An passionate, spirited audience, they seemed not to notice the autocue as she reminded them at every performance, 'I could never be here otherwise. I'm afraid of forgetting the words, which I did once in front of 135,000 people at a Central Park concert in 1968, and it's a phobia.'

She was greeted warmly upon her return to London. The audience continued to cheer her on. 'Thank you, thank you,' she said repeatedly. At the end of her final song, an oddly chosen anti-climactic rendition of 'For All We Know,' they sprang to their feet and applauded for her to return. They became hushed as she did, anticipating her to sing an encore. 'I didn't think you'd appreciate all my jokes and whatnot,' she murmured, bowed, and did not return, prompting audible cries of sadness. Nonetheless, as individuals streamed out, the general consensus was that this had been a once-in-a-lifetime experience that was well worth every penny.

Elton John, Michael Caine, and Shirley Bassey were among the many British celebrities who attended. Don Black had responded to her spedal request. 'What did you truly believe?' she inquired.

'You were fantastic,' he said. 'But the therapist thing doesn't work. We don't see psychiatrists as often over here. We sit down and have a good cup of tea and a discussion with someone, and that's how we straighten ourselves out.' She entertained her special friends after the show at the small, exclusive Blake's hotel. Streisand appeared practically ecstatic at the boisterous party, which lasted until 4 a.m. The next morning's reviews were mixed, with many critics still bemoaning the price of the tickets, the script's psychobabble, the autocue, and even the £28 price of a bottle of champagne during the interval (which did not seem to upset the ordinary public). Nonetheless, her voice received nothing but praise for its brilliance.

In the Daily Telegraph, Tony Parsons commented, "She is the supreme communicator." Only Sinatra can speak directly to the heart of an audience like Barbra Streisand. When she takes flight, she creates music that is full of memories and a sense of loss... she is without a doubt the last of the great romantics.'

London dubbed her "the ultimate pop diva." It was difficult to listen to tum on a radio station that wasn't playing her recordings. Almost every newspaper edition featured a story about her; Elton John was throwing her a £200,000 party (a much inflated figure, but it did cost nearly half that) on Sunday, 24 April, her fifty-second birthday at his country estate; she had refused to attend the 'celebrity packed' public party Sony had planned (and cancelled) the night before, much to her record company's chagrin, because she was not given control of the guest list, which would have On Monday, April 24th, Prince Charles attended the concert; Diana gave an interview from California; a full-page colour layout of Streisand and Caleigh appeared in one daily, and there was a constant barrage of stories with banners similar to 'Barbra Streisand strikes up the band's anger,' (Daily Mail, 22 April), an example of the English penchant for using a play on words. Hamlisch has only taken twelve of his main musicians to London with him. The rest of the orchestra was from the area, and they were outraged when they were requested to sign a secrecy agreement the day before the first concert, obliging them not to discuss anything related to Streisand's appearance in the press. In fact, such notes were delivered to Wembley Arena staff, as well as those at the MGM Grand, and would be at every location where she appeared.

The stage crew was not permitted to see rehearsals. 'I was instructed by my supervisor that if I see Streisand, I must turn aside because she doesn't want people gazing,' one person stated. 'It's the principle I object to, the idea that we're going to divulge material about her,' one orchestra member grumbled. I've performed for some of the world's best opera singers, but I've never heard anything so suggestive of a prima donna.'

Nonetheless, no one in the orchestra refused to sign the agreement, which was very identical to the one required of the Queen's servants. They were warned that if they did not sign, they would be replaced. This was all part of Streisand's driving demand for privacy and control, which she found especially difficult to attain when she placed herself so conspicuously in the public eye. She despised not having control over what was written about her, convinced that the truth would not be published. She desired the power, glory, renown, and seclusion afforded to non-public personalities. Since her early days as a celebrity, the media had taken control. The days of studios and publicists feeding the press at their leisure are long gone. The press was hungry for celebrity tales, and for a time, Streisand competed with Princess Diana, with photographs and stories about her, no matter how tiny, in high demand. It was as if the media felt she was too talented, famous, wealthy, and outspoken to be taken down for it.

But there is something in her demand that staff sign paperwork committing them to quiet, threatening them with dismissal if they discuss their work with her, that contradicts everything of her professed liberalism. Such techniques are not unconstitutional, but they constitute a gagging order, an infringement on others' free speech rights, while she has a forum for all of her remarks, views, and positions on many matters. The double standard is both astonishing and disheartening in this case. One would expect more from a woman like Streisand, who is constantly battling for her own personal rights.

The concert on Monday night was also a fund-raiser, with a portion of the projected £150,000 in earnings going to the Prince's Trust. Streisand last saw Charles in 1974, when he visited Hollywood. He had come to the studio where she was filming Funny Lady as she was recording the song 'So Long, Honey Lamb'. During their twenty-minute conversation, Streisand shared her mug of tea with him.

Charles is a huge fan of hers, and he seemed to adore her as a person. Members of the recording orchestra recalled seeing the two make intense eye contact. 'Sparks flew,' one musician (who asked not to be identified) noted. They met again at a champagne reception before the concert, and she warmly clasped his hand in hers twice during their five-minute conversation, neither of them appearing to be inhibited by the others present (Marvin Hamlisch, Marty Erlichman, Charles's equerries, members of the Wembley Arena management staff, and several photographers). During her performance, Charles sat in a private balcony area thirty yards from the stage with superstars such as Joan Collins and Priscilla Presley, dressed conservatively in a dark-blue suit. Streisand introduced the Disney song and remarked on her affection for songs about imaginary princes in the segment of the show where she regularly displayed video footage of Caleigh and herself and then sang 'Some Day My Prince Will Come' for the youngster. 'What makes this song extra spedal tonight is that there's a genuine one in the crowd,' she stated.

When she finished singing, Charles and the rest of the audience got to their feet and joined in a two-minute standing ovation that ended with the audience stamping their feet and demanding more. She returned to perform 'Somewhere'. When she was finished, Charles leaped to his feet again and applauded loudly. Streisand smiled heartily and made a bow gesture to him.

The sound of applause did not appease her great sense of loneliness at being away from Caleigh. 'I am devoted to my goddaughter,' she told anyone who asked about the inclusion of Caleigh's photographs in the printed programme. She called California often to speak to her. Although only on the first engagement of her tour, Streisand was already missing the child, and after the fourth and last show in London (each separated by several days as she did not like to give concerts back to back) she returned to Los Angeles expressly to see her. Then, after a joyful but short reunion, she and Erlichman rejoined Harnisch, the orchestra and her technicians in Washington DC, where the President and the First Lady attended her first-night concert there. She was fighting the beginnings of a cold, but after her Washington concerts continued on to Detroit for two concerts at the Palace of Auburn Hills arena. 'In Detroit,' she says, 'I thought, I don't know how I'm going to get through the next fifteen shows. It's very exhausting physically. It's a lot of breathing; you have to be in pretty good shape. And I don't work out vocally. I don't practise. It's the most boring thing you can imagine, doing scales. So I just said, "Fuck it, I can't [do scales]. I'm too tired the day after a concert."'

Her next venue was to be the Arrowhead Pond in Anaheim, the home of the Mighty Ducks hockey team and with 19,200 capacity the largest of all the arenas in which she had performed. By the time she arrived in Los Angeles her cold had worsened. She was suffering from viral tracheolaryngitis, placed on antibiotics and told by her doctor that she must rest her voice.

Originally scheduled for Wednesday, 25 May the first of the six Southern California concerts was postponed to Thursday, 2 June to give her a chance to recover sufficiently. The show was also scheduled to go to San Jose in northern California. A glittering array of celebrities (Michael Jackson, Warren Beatty, Goldie Hawn, Walter Matthau among them) attended opening night along with some of the most important people in her life – Elliott and Jason, Jon Peters and Caleigh, André Agassi, Don Johnson, Ray and Fran Stark, and in the front row Diana and Roslyn. As she ended her first number and came down the steps from the balcony set and walked across the front rim of the stage, she glanced down over the footlights to the front row. Diana, eighty-five and severely arthritic was on her feet applauding with the rest of the delirious crowd. Streisand leaned forward.

'Mom, you stood up. Take it easy, Mom. Sit down. I'm glad you're here. I love you,' she said, straightened, stood still for a moment and then motioned with her hands for the audience to be seated.

There was no sign of laryngitis as she launched into her programme, which now included a ten-minute Yentl sequence – 'a masterly staged affair that proved to be the most crowd-pleasing sequence of the show'. She received even greater acclamation at the finish. 'One sensed it was for more than the music,' Robert Hilburn of the Los Angeles Times wrote, 'It was also in admiration of the independence and determination Streisand has shown over the years in such pursuits as film directing.'

Since London she had also changed the ending of the concert, which had been the melancholy song 'For All We Know' about the possibility of two people never meeting again, to the brighter more uplifting 'Somewhere', from West Side Story.

'If there's such a thing as a concert ticket that's worth the money, this might be the one,' Daily Variety declared. She played the second concert on 4 June, but – her throat still giving her problems – the last four shows were cancelled. As the Arrowhead Pond was booked ahead for several weeks, it was decided she would return to Anaheim after San Jose and New York to end the tour with concerts there, on 10, 18, 22 and 24 July.

Her throat problems were cured by the time she opened at Madison Square Garden on Monday night, June 20 for the first of five concerts. The majority of theatres are dark on Monday and almost all Broadway's current performers turned out to welcome her home. She was, after all, a Brooklyn girl, one of their own. Attending her triumphant return were Liza Minnelli, Chita Rivera and the casts from almost every show along the Great White Way. She seemed relaxed, looked marvellous (she had fresh copies of her two gowns made for each dty on the tour) and was in magnificent voice. She had returned to the New York concert stage the same week that the city played host to the Gay Games. 'One of the best things about the games', she told her enthusiastic audience, 'is that I can walk down the street and not be recognised because there are so many impersonators.'

She told Liza over the microphone after singing 'The Man Who Got Away,' 'Your mom sang that fantastic.' Rex Reed remarked that it was the epitome of chutzpah, but Liza smiled and did not appear to take the statement personally.

Reed was not totally won over, despite the cheering and stamping crowd in the Gardens. 'There's no questioning her talent,' he continues, 'but it's always the voice, not the interpretation, that gets to you. Every inflection, modulation, and supersonic high note appears to be recorded on vinyl. You could be listening to records at home. She lacks the sensitivity of Garland or Piaf, as well as the kind of spontaneous self-discovery that develops the art of spontaneity. She's such a perfectionist... she's not going to let you in.'

Reed was the outlier. It's nearly impossible to compare Streisand to Garland or Piaf. Both victims, presenting their scarred, fragile selves to audiences who listened to them in a far different way than Streisand's audiences listen to her. Streisand's followers do not share her pain; instead, they celebrate her courage in overcoming all of the difficulties she appears to have surmounted - converting homely into beautiful, ethnic into mainstream, and daring to enter a man's world as director, producer, and business executive. She is a classy feminist, a liberal who is proud of the term and is never afraid to express herself. And, with the exception of Frank Sinatra, she has maintained continuous celebrity and appeal for longer years than any other entertainment personality. She is significantly smarter than Garland or Piaf and approaches her work in a more academic manner. They were undoubtedly one-of-a-kind, and they could move you to tears and chills, making you want to jump up on stage and take them in your arms, to save them. In Garland's case, forgive anything and everything, even if she couldn't hit the notes or recall the lyrics. Much more is expected of Streisand, and she ensures that she will live up to her own, lofty standards to the best of her ability.

The tour, together with her multimedia endeavours, had given her more star power than any other concert performer, rock star or opera diva. And by the time she finished all of the performances, with two shows added to her Madison Square Gardens engagements, she would have made the most money in entertainment history. 'Let me say this, I have a long way to go,' she told Barbara Walters the previous December, before appearing in Las Vegas. I still have a lot to learn. I'm still vulnerable to criticism. I go through phases where I can simply laugh at it. And there are times when I think it's just plain mean. Life must be accepted for what it is. The agony and the ecstasy; the hatred and the love. My musical director [Hamlisch] came to meet me and gave me a book on changing the world called Life Is the Message. We can't, after all, change the world. It's an enormous task, but by changing ourselves, all of us can affect the world in a very little way.'

The tour had helped her overcome her dread of performing in front of a live audience, while the demons remained, albeit less active, but had she altered the world in any way? Certainly not, despite the fact that she had transformed public tastes, their perception of beauty, the notion that without a formal education, you could not walk as an equal with intellectuals, and the notion that women were not emotionally prepared to stand toe to toe with male power brokers. By doing things her way, the tour, which included a stop in Las Vegas, had grossed more than $64 million.1 She made all of the final decisions, from the music to the screenplay to the performance, set, sound, merchandise, and road arrangements. Her efforts were total, as was the only way she knew how to work. She always dealt from strength to strength. This was not a 'comeback' tour like so many of Garland's before it. Streisand was a big star despite being unavailable to the public for so long.

'She's God's bell,' says one of her staunchest supporters, exercise guru Richard Simmons. 'I weighed 200 pounds in eighth grade. And I witnessed her transformation from not the most beautiful girl in the world to the most beautiful woman I've ever seen in my life. She improved my self-esteem.'

Her own self-image was a different story. Nothing ever seemed to be enough. She had to prove herself time and time again. It had become an obsession. Something inside her ate at her and spurred her on. No one who worked with her could ever keep up with her. She returned to Los Angeles in mid-July 1994 to finish the four Arrowhead Pond concerts. Rumours had circulated that she would cancel. The weather was excessively hot and humid. She was having difficulties with her throat once more. She did, in fact, appear, much to the delight of her audience. On the final night, Hollywood came out in force, with many of the people who had previously attended her concerts in Las Vegas, New York, or California returning to hear her again. She received standing ovations from the moment she took the stage. After the final song, she asked the audience if they wanted to stay and watch her perform for the television cameras. As the bulk hurried back to their seats, there was a scramble.

Friends and VIP guests were ushered backstage to an airless, white-walled chamber to wait for Streisand and pay their respects. They sat restlessly as they watched her on the big screen, hearing 'that crystalline voice rising, rising - and then, at the break where virtually every other singer becomes reedy, blazing higher so that you feel [as Marvin Hamlisch describes it], that she's carried you through'. Warren Beatty wrapped his arm around a tired and heavily pregnant Annette Bening. Elliott and Jason were there with Diana, who was in a wheelchair, and Shirley MacLaine spoke to her while squatting in an Indian fashion. (Despite being brother and sister, Beatty and MacLaine rarely attend events together.) Despite the late hour, Caleigh remained calmly alongside her father. The screen eventually went blank. It was late and the filming session had ended. A select group of those waiting were led into Streisand's adjoining white carpeted, heavily mirrored dressing room, which had silver-framed portraits of Jason and Caleigh.

'You did well,' Diana said grudgingly. 'I'm very proud of you.'

Streisand, still looking lovely and fresh, replied, 'Thanks, mom,' her words said so softly she could hardly be heard.

By eleven o'clock the next morning, she was at Sony Studios, editing video for the television special and mixing tracks for a planned CD of the concert (actually an accretion of multiple concerts). Home Box Office anticipated that the televised concert, like the tour, would break viewership records. She promised she'd never undertake another tour again. 'You must put on make-up and comb your hair. You must wear high heels. 'My feet cramp!' she grumbled.

As soon as she got off the road, Streisand got back to work on The Margarethe Cammermeyer Story, which is now being developed as a television film called Serving in Silence. She started Serving in Silence in the fall of 1992 after reading a newspaper article about Lieutenant-Colonel Cammermeyer, a highly distinguished Army nurse for twenty-six years who had been discharged for divulging her sexual orientation during a security-clearance interview. She had been a leader in the struggle to remove the military's ban on gays, having been the highest-ranking military official ever fired for homosexuality.

'Barbra had a strong desire to do this project,' Cis Corman stated. 'It was such a glaring case of prejudice and discrimination.' Convincing the Colonel to make a film of her story was difficult, even for Streisand. Finally, she agreed, and Streisand moved forward with producers Craig Zadan (a former close friend of Stephen Sondheim) and Neil Meron, who had produced the Emmy-nominated Gypsy starring Bette Midler, while she remained executive producer. The production required a star to play the Colonel. Glenn Close had recently left the Sunset Boulevard cast in Los Angeles and had some free time before the November premiere in New York in the spring of 1994. Streisand was on her way to England. Close, she thought, would be excellent in the character, giving both the strength and the feminine elements of Cammermeyer. Close, one of Hollywood's finest actors, agreed to join the project as both a star and a co-executive producer alongside Streisand. The two women hit it off right away, and a writer was hired and the business was launched.

On the surface, presenting a huge story about lesbians on the small screen appeared impossible. Advertisers were hesitant to acquire time because of fears of a viewer boycott. The power of Streisand and Close's involvement, however, was enough for Lindy DeKoven, NBC's senior vice-president of mini-series and feature films for television, to accept the idea.

'What the network requested and what it got were two different things,' said Craig Zadan. 'The network anticipated it would mostly feature courtroom scenes. But what emerged during the writing process was a love story. "Under no circumstances are you to remove any of this love story," Glenn said. Otherwise, I won't have anything to play as an actress."' The script was not as violent as what was proposed for The Normal Heart, but it did include moving moments of two lesbians kissing and embracing.

When Streisand concluded her tour, the film was being shot on location in Vancouver, Canada. A group in New York called the Family Defense Council had already threatened a boycott of advertisers unless the lesbian kiss was removed. Judy Davis, Close's co-star, was threatening to depart, believing that her role would be sacrificed to appease the hostile group.

Not only was Streisand working on the contentious Serving in Silence, but she was also rewriting The Normal Heart with Larry Kramer and The Mirror Has Two Faces with Richard LaGravenese. The final appeared to be morphing into a commercial property, one that would not offer as many issues as the Kramer vehicle did. Despite her devotion to The Normal Heart, she really wanted to be able to demonstrate to a studio that she could execute a modest commercial film on budget and on schedule. Kramer, on the other hand, lacked time. Mirror would be harder to cope with if he went into production first. She didn't want this to happen, nor did she want to lose The Normal Heart. She was going to have to juggle the two in order to placate Kramer. Streisand, on the other hand, appeared to have walked directly into the eye of a hurricane.

'I'm a shy person,' she told an interviewer for the Los Angeles Times who inquired if she had plans for another tour, 'and I don't have to go out on the road again. I lost weight and slept better. I was afraid I would let people down, that I wouldn't be good enough. Everything worked out in the end. It was necessary for me to achieve this confidence in order to feel completely at peace onstage, to believe that I belonged and deserved to be there, and that I could offer and accept the love of those audiences. I am truly grateful to those individuals. I didn't enjoy my own singing for much too long... But it's not my passion; my passion is making movies.'

The process of filmmaking, the concept that she could create people, live, and realise her ideals, had captivated her since her first days on Funny Girl with Willie Wyler. As an actress, she could play Fanny

Brice, but the concept was Wyler's. Being able to act as both producer and director, as she had in Yentl and The Prince of Tides, had allowed her more control over the script, money, and production. She made the big decisions, chose material that personally involved her, could make a statement or live out a fantasy, but she had to be highly motivated and the tale and characters must be crystal obvious to her. She was not the only actor-director out there. Clint Eastwood, Mel Gibson, Kenneth Branagh, and Jodie Foster all starred in significant films directed by themselves, and none experienced the same level of criticism as Streisand. Rejection and criticism hurt her severely since she valued recognition and approval so much.

Columbia was glad she opted to work on a commercial production like The Mirror Has Two Faces. The part she was to portray was comparable to Katie Morosky in The Way We Were, the clever lady, plain on the outside but with inner beauty, who wins the affection of the attractive hero after a struggle. Without success, she had pressed Arthur Laurents for years to come up with a story concept for a sequel. For a time, Robert Redford possessed the rights and had been equally passionate, approaching Laurents with little success. She now had an idea with a similar theme and the same commercial potential. She told the press, "I think I'm always drawn to films about the mystery of appearances." 'The Mirror Has Two Faces' is a delightful love story. It does, however, have serious undertones regarding vanity and beauty, the exterior vs the internal.'

While she was on tour, LaGravenese sent her his first amended draft. She thought it went in the wrong direction and requested him to revise it. When she received this version, she decided she preferred the earlier one, despite the fact that it needed more work. After several weeks of unsatisfactory story discussions with LaGravenese, she called in Carrie Fisher, who had successfully adapted her novel Postcards from the Edge for the movie, hoping Fisher could bring her character to life. Streisand returned to LaGravenese with more comprehensive recommendations, and he began work on what would become the final shooting screenplay because Fisher's compensation for the work was higher than the budget permitted.

The Normal Heart was put on hold once more, and she was torn between Kramer's rage and her own guilt. She not only adored the concept, but she also sympathised with Kramer's physical condition, particularly his fear of dying before the film was completed. Jason had a good buddy in Kramer, and as one of the country's leading gay campaigners, he nearly always received press coverage when he chose to speak out on any relevant matter. She knew he'd be enraged that she was postponing the project yet again and would not remain mute in his complaint. She expected trouble, and it arrived just as The Mirror Has Two Faces was unveiled as her next project.

'Why are you doing this nonsense?' Kramer yelled at her when she informed him of her plans, unable to control his rage.

'It's not a shithole!'

'It's a load of shit. Everyone I know thinks it's a load of garbage.'

'Who said it was a shithole?'

'Well, Jason said it's a shithole.'

'Jason thinks it's a shithole?'

'Yes. He did.'

Kramer noted, "She seemed suddenly reflective, and I pressed my point." "This is the pinnacle of your life." "You don't have two years to squander your time, energy, and intelligence on a piece of shit," I added. "That's not how you create a great body of work." I hated having to hurt her because she was troubled.

"I've already created a great body of work!" she exclaimed. "I've tried so hard not to be too hard on myself. What are you doing to me? I'd like to make a film without going through so much upheaval. I want to do it as an exercise to show that I can go in, make a video quickly, without driving everyone insane, including myself, and then go out and on to the next one. Anyway, everyone is putting pressure on me to do it."

' "No one has more power than you."

'"That's what you believe. It is not simple. "I said I'd do it, and Jeff Bridges [the actor who was supposed to play opposite her] will kill me."

' "Why don't you send him the script of The Normal Heart?"

' "Oh, he'd be wonderful, but I couldn't do that!"

'They don't live in the real world in Hollywood,' Kramer said after relaying this story. 'As a result, she booked The Mirror Has Two Faces first, with The Normal Heart following after.'

Meanwhile, Serving in Silence was being edited for television, and she was personally involved in the final product. 'I would like people to relate with the persons in the story [the Colonel and her lesbian girlfriend],' she said to the press, despite previously expressing her belief that there were significant disparities between heterosexuals and homosexuals. We're more alike than we are different.' She got along great with Glenn Close, whom she admired for her "dignity and integrity." The show wasn't supposed to air for another ten weeks, but the press was already writing scathing articles about it, stating that the network only agreed to do it because of Streisand and Close's involvement and because they would then be able to re-screen Streisand's HBO concert special.

'Why is it that every time I read something written about her [Streisand], it always has some negative connotation?' Colonel Cammermeyer wondered. What is it about her being creative, enriching, compassionate, and giving of herself emotionally and financially to causes she believes in that is so irritating to people?' Cammermeyer saw a comparison between her own experience as a lesbian in the military; both worlds are dominated by guys' clubs that close ranks against women who don't toe the line'.

Serving in Silence premiered on NBC on February 6, 1995, to generally positive reviews and strong viewership. It was nominated for Emmys in seven categories, including Best Original Film Made for Television and Best Actress, but did not win. When her work in movies was overlooked for Oscars, Streisand was always unhappy and resentful. Her energy and excitement, however, had been channelled into the development of Mirror by this time, but she kept working with Kramer on The Normal Heart and seeking to secure money and a celebrity to act alongside her so that the picture could be scheduled to follow Mirror. Kramer, whom she actually admired and cared for, was placated for the time being.

In November 1994, she was preoccupied with fund-raising for California Democrats running for state or national office, not concerts, but luncheons and galas at which she was a celebrity guest, along with a slew of others. When Prince Charles landed in Los Angeles for the first time in twenty years, she took a break from her political efforts to attend a banquet in his honour. They just had a few minutes to converse, but a close observer remarked on their "terrific eye contact." It sounded like a Pow!' Charles was staying at the Bel Air Hotel in Stone Canyon, which runs through the mountains above Sunset Boulevard in West Los Angeles. The hotel resembled a French rural château, with its beautiful grounds, eleven acres of private parkland, ancient trees, and exquisite artificial lake - home to a bevy of swans - and the stunning rooms reflected this concept. Charles organised a private rendezvous in his opulent suite of rooms a few days after Charles and Streisand spoke at the event, where they spent an hour alone together.

A few pressmen had gathered at the front gates by this time, having heard about her coming. Streisand hurried into a waiting automobile, hair flying in the chilly November wind, head down, large black glasses obscuring her face, belted coat and high boots on, and whizzed away. Streisand and Charles ever being romantically involved felt strange enough to make sense. True, Charles is a fan, and they got along well when they met, although briefly, in London during her tour. But there was more than a hint of romance in the secrecy and the lack of other participants at the meeting to pique the media's curiosity.

As Christmas 1994 arrived, she still didn't have a significant partner in her life. She kept in touch with Peter Jennings and sought his counsel on political issues that affected her, things she read about in the papers and wanted to know more about. Jennings possessed charm, warmth, intelligence, and his own sphere of celebrity. But he was also dating Katherine Freed, a younger, very attractive television producer.

Why couldn't she meet a soulmate, a man who would deeply love her and to whom she could return the depth of that love? She was no longer the fame-hungry girl who had married and divorced Elliott, or the smitten woman who had given herself totally to Peters and then let the making of a film tear them apart. She'd met, worked with, and had affairs with some of the world's most powerful, dynamic, bright, and sexy men. So yet, no man she had been drawn to had measured up to the best of those gentlemen. The man she desired would not be scared by her enormous popularity or her unwavering dedication to whatever she achieved. He must share her enthusiasms, convictions, and expectations, as well as have a successful profession on his own. He also had to be compassionate and understanding when appropriate, as well as tough and protective when necessary. He couldn't be married or have 'a roving eye'. Such a man was difficult to come by. But she never gave up hope that he was still out there.

Streisand had committed to give a lecture on 'The Artist as Citizen' on 3 February 1995 at Harvard's John F. Kennedy School of Government, and she was taking notes all the while on what she intended to say, which was mostly a defence of Hollywood celebrities' right to speak out on politics. She had been agitating over the matter for months, having witnessed the media's discrimination against politically engaged members of the film colony during the presidential election. She flew to New York the week before the address to consult with Jennings. Her greatest dread was not the speech itself, but the question-and-answer period that would follow, during which she would be asked to react on issues or matters about which she was insufficiently versed. Jennings served as a consultant but did not rewrite her speech.

Ivy League academia was ecstatic about her upcoming presentation at Harvard, with much more focus on her than on Secretary of State Warren Christopher's recent visit to the school. Because of the high demand for tickets in the 700-seat auditorium, the Institute of Politics had to run a lottery. It was decided to set up a camera news pool to cover her televised presence. Cambridge police were stationed at every door and stairs, and special equipment was built to check for bogus tickets. Even though no incidents of suspected violence occurred throughout her performance tour, Streisand remained scared of an attack or shooting by some mad individual.

She arrived in Boston by private plane two days before her speech with her assistant, Kim Skalecki, and was driven to the Charles Hotel, where she was given the presidential suite. That night, she stayed in her room, reworking her speech yet more. The next day, she had a 'great lunch' with John F. Kennedy Jr. and twenty-five ardent, serious, idealistic students, during which she discussed topics ranging from welfare to defence spending. When the youthfully gorgeous Kennedy met her earlier and accompanied her on a tour of Harvard, she became teary-eyed. Her memorable visit with his father was thirty-one years ago. Later, she audited a constitutional law class, for which she even completed the assignment after rehearsing her speech in the unoccupied theatre.

Her anxieties grew more as the moment came for her to speak. She waited in the wings after the audience had been seated for a lengthy laudatory introduction by Harvard University's interim president, Albert Carnesale. She was really apprehensive when she eventually took the platform, which had previously hosted Mikhail S. Gorbachev, Newt Gingrich, Al Gore, and a slew of presidential candidates and administration officials. Wearing a conservative charcoal-grey pin-striped, severely tailored Donna Karan dress, a single strand of pearls, and seriously sculptured' nails, she clasped and unclasped her hands, hugged her knees, rocked backwards and forwards, and clenched the arms of her chair as Carnesale talked about her achievements.

When she eventually took the microphone, she asked, 'You heard of shpilkes?' in a Brooklyn accent, to a roar of laughter and loud applause. She sounded much like the impassioned Katie Morosky in The Way We Were as she told the students, 'I must admit I'm confused by [House Speaker Newt Gingrich's] thinking.' She was standing in front of a large wall hanging with Harvard University - John F. Kennedy School of Government and the school's emblem emblazoned on it. He recommends removing children from the homes of impoverished moms and placing them in orphanages. If that's an example of mainstream culture, I'm glad to be a part of the counterculture. I'm also pleased to be a liberal. What's the deal with that these days? The liberals were liberators; they opposed slavery, fought for women's suffrage, fought against Hitler and Stalin, fought to end segregation, and fought to end apartheid. Liberals abolished child labour and instituted the five-day work week! 'What is there to be ashamed of?' She shrugged her shoulders and spread her palms palm up, as if to say, "You know what I mean?"

Defending a celebrity's right to participate in politics, she said, "What is the sin?" Is it concerned with your country? Why should the actor relinquish his citizenship merely because he works in show business? Tom Hanks had to learn a lot about being a homosexual man with AIDS for his role in the film Philadelphia. Should he have kept quiet about this? For the past three decades, Paul Newman has been an ardent advocate of civil freedoms as well as a big philanthropist. Is it preferable if he just produced money and played golf? Is Robert Redford a moron because he knows more about the environment than most members of Congress? ... Because we have to walk in other people's shoes and live in other people's skins, most artists seem on the humanist, sympathetic side of public discourse. This does tend to make us more amenable to more tolerant policies,' she happily said.

She went on to accuse the far right of "waging a war for the soul of America by making art a partisan issue," with her eyes looking down from time to time to check her notes. She stated that because the arts program was so little ('the Public Broadcasting System costs each taxpayer less than one dollar per year,' it couldn't be attacked for financial reasons. Perhaps it's about closing artists' thoughts and lips who could have anything thought-provoking to say.' She recalled memories from her childhood, such as how her father walked home from his teaching profession to deposit the money he had saved in the pushke, the charity box that many Jews kept in their homes. She cited her own experience as a member of Erasmus High School's Choral Club, emphasising how crucial it was for youngsters everywhere to "find solace in an instrument to play or a canvas to paint on," urging the government not to slash such necessary expenditures.

Throughout her fifty-minute speech, she appeared enthusiastic and edgy at the same time. She made a lot of gestures, pushed her shoulder-length, blonde-streaked hair away from her face, wet her lips, and drank water whenever she paused. She received a standing ovation during her closing words. Carnesale took the floor and indicated that there would be a brief break before their visitor answered questions. Backstage, Streisand appeared tense and needed to be comforted. The dreaded question period followed.

Her return to the podium was met with a round of applause.

The first question was posed by Christopher Garda, a Harvard senior. 'Why are you being so defensive?' he asked, adding that the artistic community appeared to be "out of touch with society."

Streisand raised her hands in a move that appeared to say, "I'll answer that." He was bombarded with hisses. 'How come you're a Republican?' she asked.

Her dissatisfaction with this segment of the show developed as the questions became more technical rather than philosophical. 'I don't know enough about that to give you an answer,' she replied several times. When asked if she had any political ambitions, she responded, 'Political ambition and political passion are two different things.' With only one more inquiry allowed, a young woman congratulated her for being articulate, rich, and intelligent. Streisand smiled at her with a crooked Fanny Brice grin. 'Do you have a guy for me?' she inquired.

She'd placed herself on the front lines. She was always creating difficult goals for herself, a higher mountain to climb, a fresh set of challenges to accomplish, and critics to persuade. The press mostly praised her look and speech, but arch-conservative author Arianna Huffington responded with a blistering reply in the Washington Post. 'How could anyone hear anything over the racket of such high-pitched melodrama, Barbra?' she demanded. 'Why do you insist on misrepresenting conservatives' desire to reduce taxpayer-funded arts subsidies as motivated by "disrespect" for art and artists? Is your desire to reduce the defence budget motivated by "disrespect" for our military and its personnel?' Her proposal was for the business sector to raise the $167 million yearly budget required to sustain the arts.

Streisand was unconcerned by Huffington's rant since she had little regard for her. She had spoken up on matters that were important to her and believed she had a right to speak in public.

By the end of the summer, she was overwhelmed by pre-production pressures for Mirror, which would be shot in and around New York in late October. Casting had been a fairly easy process. Pierce Brosnan, the suave, handsome Irishman, fresh from his role as James Bond in the most recent 007 film, was cast as the devilishly attractive other man (in this case Streisand's movie brother-in-law), Dudley Moore as Bridges's drinking buddy, and Lauren Bacall as Streisand's glamorous mother.

'Everyone was upbeat on the first day of shooting,' a crew member recalled. 'I've worked with Barbra on a number of different film projects, and she appeared calmer and more assured. I've known her for at least thirty years and have witnessed her transformation. Of course, we all do over such a long period of time. But the transformation in Barbra's life has been as profound as everything else in her life. She's lost touch with reality and only sees things from her perspective. She's always been self-centred, demanding, and a workaholic. But she used to have a fantastic zest for life, wanting to devour the entire globe. That is no longer present. I believe she has lost her sense of humour, her capacity to laugh at herself. She's been taking herself far too seriously lately.

'She's always been like that little girl with the curl in the centre of her brow - one day she's fantastic, the next she's a jerk; she can be your closest friend and sympathetic supporter. Then the wind shifts, and she can cut you off in the most heinous, horrible way. I've seen it happen with frightening regularity in recent years. It became a typical occurrence on the set of Mirror. I was scared that what I was witnessing was the complete unravelling of someone I had deeply loved and revered. The filming procedure itself was reminiscent of a lousy movie. "Where is all this going, and what is it all about?" I wondered. She developed paranoia. There was no disputing what she said. She was the only one on the planet. It was megalomania on steroids. I cried when I returned to the apartment I was staying in while we were in New York. It was as if I had lost someone extremely close to me.'

She had expected this project to be significantly less complicated or emotional than The Normal Heart. It was meant to be the film that demonstrated to studios that she could make a non-musical, commercial film on a shoestring budget, proving that she was a dependable, bankable filmmaker. She realised she had made a mistake when she cast Dudley Moore in his role one week into filming. He was too funny, too much Arthur the drunk, which shifted the focus of the moment he was in.

'It was difficult to determine if he was playing an inebriated character or if he was actually one,' one crew member observed. 'One thing was certain: Barbra and Moore were incompatible, despite the fact that she was the producer, star, and director.'

Moore was shortly replaced by George Segal, with whom Streisand had previously collaborated on The Owl and the Pussycat. Then, just before Christmas, Dante Spinotti and his eight-man crew were replaced by Andrzej Bartkowiak, who had previously worked with her on Nuts, and new technicians. This was a significant shift. The tone of the film is set by the director of photography. Streisand was dissatisfied with her appearance in the daily rushes or with the shots that Spinotti had captured. 'She had been moaning about the camera work nearly from the start of the filming,' one set member stated. 'There were far too many gauzes wrapped around the lens. Her eyes, which were one of her better characteristics, became quite soft.'

Two days later, she fired Oscar-winning film editor Alan Heim and replaced him with Jeff Werner, who had previously worked with her. The winter months were very harsh. Exterior shooting had to be postponed, while interior sets had to be built in overtime hours. A film that was originally budgeted for $35 million dollars quickly ballooned by several millions, much to the chagrin of studio management. Streisand was tense, and the set was buzzing with anxiety. Cis Corman, the co-producer, was more diplomatic than

Streisand and worked hard to keep the principal cast and crew members on good terms with Streisand. Even Jeff Bridges, who is known for his easy going personality, found her challenging. '[She] can irritate you, but if I get irritated, I can't work. So I don't let myself get there,' he explained at the time.

Outsiders were not permitted on the set. When they were shooting a scene at a store or restaurant, the area was cordoned off and guards patrolled with walkie-talkies. 'The entire team [actor, director of photography, staff, security] is a walking thermometer for You Know Who,' said one onlooker. 'The word would pass - she's feeling fine... she's applying make-up... she's left the trailer... she's due shortly... she's on her way.'

On a rare January morning, New York Post entertainment reporter Cindy Adams was granted access to the set, an indoor antiques and collectible bazaar on 25th Street that had been turned into a 'Annual Antique Spring Market' for the scene being shot. (Streisand had previously cased it and purchased various pieces for the penthouse.) This meant that the performers had to dress in light spring attire in the midst of New York's winter freeze - the coldest, snowiest January in fifty years. The crew arrived at 5 a.m. to put up lights and camera angles, as well as to decorate the walls with early American quilts. Streisand arrived at 9 a.m. in a little pink cardigan and immediately altered the lights, camera angles, and whatever else that could be rearranged. 'At her side was Renata, her gorgeous assistant with lovely blonde hair,' Adams explained.

Streisand was to be seen scrutinising an early American patchwork quilt in a wall showcase while Segal asked Bridges about his sex life with his mousey wife, 'So, did you do it already?'

By the time lunch arrived, Streisand had not yet approved of the scene. She was watching the dailies and writing notes for the next day's work at 9 p.m. that evening, having had a sandwich for dinner, completely absorbed with the movie she was making, fighting to bring it to life as she envisioned it. Mirror now belonged only to her. She was completely immersed. She got home at 11 p.m., studied her lines for the next day's scenes, fell asleep weary, and was up and working on them again by 7 a.m.

She was so preoccupied with the development of Mirror that she had forgotten that her option on The Normal Heart, which she had never given up believing in, had expired on January 2nd. When Kramer's representative pressured her for a decision on whether to renew her contract or let Kramer take it elsewhere, she remained silent. Finally, as April neared, with Mirror still shooting and overages piling up, Streisand insisted on making The Normal Heart once her current obligation was completed and she had signed a male star and a director, having determined she would not direct herself. Jason called Kramer and offered himself as director if Kramer could persuade his mother that he could do it. Kramer had hoped for a more experienced filmmaker and thought this was a bad idea.

Then, on 8 April, Kramer, who had still had no further word on whether Streisand would pick up her option, was interviewed by Variety in an article that was reprinted and excerpted widely: 'This woman has had this play since 1986, She doesn't own it any more and my health is deteriorating and I would very much like to see the movie made while I'm alive. She had planned to make The Normal Heart, a film about a worldwide plague, but she changed her mind at the last minute to make a film about a woman who has a facelift. I didn't believe it was right of her to do that to me, her LGBT fans, and the people with AIDS about whom she speaks so movingly.' 'My ten-year futile struggle with Barbra to film The Normal Heart has been almost as long as my fight as an AIDS campaigner to eliminate this plague,' he continued.

'I am terribly conscious of the ticking clock,' Streisand said in a public statement. As a result, I am stepping down and will no longer be affiliated with the project. I wish Larry the best of luck in getting The Normal Heart made.1 I am personally committed to programs that reflect and advance the needs of the gay community.'

'Barbra was very wounded by Larry's attitude and the terrible public attention she received over the now-abandoned property,' said a close friend. 'I believe The Normal Heart was almost as essential to her as Yentl was. And Larry had made an indelible impression on her, raising her awareness of both the epidemic and the LGBT community. But when he went public, she turned cold on him. She believed she had contributed nearly as much to the project as he had, and that he should have realised how much she cared and how much it meant to her. She saw it as a personal attack.'

On April 15, she faxed Kramer, accusing him of being self-destructive, acting unreasonable, and asking too much for himself while she had not been compensated for the many years she had worked on the film. 'I adore this project - and I was striving to get it done... for your sake and mine... I have to finish Mirror just as you asked me to finish Heart.' Then she begged him to stop saying Mirror was a movie about a woman with a facelift, and she requested him to read the script before passing judgement.

After the fight over The Normal Heart, at least two members of the crew gave anonymous statements to the press about the difficulties on the set and Streisand's frenetic behaviour, tantrums, and general ill-humour. There were ultimatums issued. No one was to speak to the press or their careers would be jeopardised. 'This is my first major film,' said one associate. 'I'm terrified to death. She has the ability to make it difficult, if not impossible, for me to do another TriStar project, and given the frenzied manner she has been acting, I have little doubt she would if she knew I was talking to you. I walk out on the set every day and can't believe what I'm seeing and hearing. There is a black cloud of fear, apprehension, and a desire for the filming to cease. But, just when we believed that was going to happen, she decides she needs to reshoot a crucial section. That's another five to seven days' worth of work, not to mention the set reconstruction. When the last shoot is finished, I know I'm going to turn off my phones and pager and sleep for four days. Barbra? She has a summer ahead of her to supervise the editing, then the advertising and marketing campaign, as well as the release and distribution. And she isn't going to let go of this film until she has driven everyone involved in post-production insane.'

'I love Barbra,' says Richard LaGravenese in her defence. She is greatly vilified and misunderstood.'

'Be cautious of your wishes; they may come true,' Stephen Sondheim wrote. Streisand has always wanted for more than she has, whether it's a better profession, more money, more success, or more love.

Streisand aspired to be a great star, which she achieved, but only with her continual focus on what she was doing and how she could reach her goal. With Elizabeth Taylor, she is one of just two giant Hollywood survivors, albeit the only one still in the filmmaking business. Unlike Taylor, she has not had to deal with drugs, obesity, several divorces, tragedy, or serious and frequent illness. She does not move her followers to tears or her friends to form protective shields around her. Her greatest victories are not in the distant past. Taylor was forced to invent herself, make herself over, sell the world on what and who she was, and she is still in there selling, pushing, without her natural, breathtaking beauty, a mother to goad her, or anyone to guide her.

'You just push, push, push and never let up,' Barbara Walters told her once.

'I push because I want things to be better,' she said.

Pushy, hungry, grasping, brilliant, possessor of one of the greatest popular voices of her era, dazzling in her accomplishments, infuriating in her absolute refusal to change her personality or beliefs to please anyone other than herself, Streisand is a living kaleidoscope of the latter half of the twentieth century. She represents so many important aspects of our existence. Remember the young Streisand as the homely Fanny Brice, looking into the mirror and singing, 'I'm the Greatest Star,' with sassy confidence? Remember how she stood next to the stunning Ingrid Bergman at the Academy Awards, clad in a daring, see-through gown, clutching Oscar tightly in her grasp and exclaiming, 'Hullo, Gorgeous!' Consider that wonderful cinematic moment in The Way We Were, when the handsomest man in Hollywood, Robert Redford, took her in his arms and tears streamed down her face. She was the ordinary girl who might become beautiful, and she continues to inspire most of us to believe that anything can be won, even against the odds, if you have the courage and vision to see it through.

Call it chutzpah, guts, or strength; Streisand defines it all. She has also ventured to venture beyond the ordinary into the daring extreme, both off and on screen. She used her heritage to her advantage, emulated style, and possessed a voice that has never become reedy or plummeted into tobacco or alcoholic huskiness. It's a voice that carries us along with it as it soars. It comes from deep inside her, given to her by her special god, possibly to compensate for the things she lacked - a father, beauty, inner serenity; a voice that can only occur once.

The contents of this book may not be copied, reproduced or transmitted without the express written permission of the author or publisher. Under no circumstances will the publisher or author be responsible or liable for any damages, compensation or monetary loss arising from the information contained in this book, whether directly or indirectly. .

Disclaimer Notice:

Although the author and publisher have made every effort to ensure the accuracy and completeness of the content, they do not, however, make any representations or warranties as to the accuracy, completeness, or reliability of the content. , suitability or availability of the information, products, services or related graphics contained in the book for any purpose. Readers are solely responsible for their use of the information contained in this book

Every effort has been made to make this book possible. If any omission or error has occurred unintentionally, the author and publisher will be happy to acknowledge it in upcoming versions.

Printed in Great Britain
by Amazon

35127141R00076